SIMPLY INSTITUTIONAL ETHNOGRAPHY

Creating a Sociology for People

Dorothy E. Smith and Alison I. Griffith

Institutional ethnography (IE) originated as a feminist alternative to sociologies defining people as the objects of study. Instead, IE explores the social relations that dominate the life of the particular subject in focus.

Simply Institutional Ethnography is written by two pioneers in the field and grounded in decades of ground-breaking work. Dorothy Smith and Alison Griffith lay out the basics of how institutional ethnography proceeds as a sociology. The book introduces the concepts – Discourse, Work, Text – that institutional ethnographers have found to be key ideas used to organize what they learn from the study of people's experience. *Simply Institutional Ethnography* builds an ethnography that makes this material visible as coordinated sequences of social relations that reach beyond the particularities of local experience. In explicating the foundations of IE and its principal concepts, *Simply Institutional Ethnography* reflects on the ways in which the field may move forward.

(Institutional Ethnography)

DOROTHY E. SMITH is an adjunct professor in the Department of Sociology at the University of Victoria.

ALISON I. GRIFFITH was a professor emerita in the Faculty of Education at York University.

INSTITUTIONAL ETHNOGRAPHY: STUDIES IN THE SOCIAL ORGANIZATION OF KNOWLEDGE

Series editor: Eric Mykhalovskiy

Institutional Ethnography: Studies in the Social Organization of Knowledge is a groundbreaking series that brings together prominent scholars from around the world who engage with institutional ethnography in a range of ways. Books in the series promote excellence and innovation in institutional ethnographic inquiry while strengthening interdisciplinary dialogue between institutional ethnography and related forms of research. In a world being shaped by accelerated interconnection, this venue for exploring how ruling relations are created and operate, how they affect people's day-to-day's lives, and how they can be transformed will make a lasting and meaningful impact on the field.

Simply Institutional Ethnography

Creating a Sociology for People

DOROTHY E. SMITH AND ALISON I. GRIFFITH

UNIVERSITY OF TORONTO PRESS
Toronto Buffalo London

ISBN 978-1-4875-2805-8 (cloth)   ISBN 978-1-4875-2808-9 (EPUB)
ISBN 978-1-4875-2806-5 (paper)   ISBN 978-1-4875-2807-2 (PDF)

Institutional Ethnography: Studies in the Social Organization of Knowledge

Library and Archives Canada Cataloguing in Publication

Title: Simply institutional ethnography : creating a sociology for people /
    Dorothy E. Smith and Alison I. Griffith.
Names: Smith, Dorothy E., 1926– author. | Griffith, Alison I., author.
Description: Series statement: Institutional ethnography: studies in the social
    organization of knowledge | Includes bibliographical references and index.
Identifiers: Canadiana (print) 20210369078 | Canadiana (ebook) 20210369108 |
    ISBN 9781487528058 (cloth) | ISBN 9781487528065 (paper) |
    ISBN 9781487528089 (EPUB) | ISBN 9781487528072 (PDF)
Subjects: LCSH: Ethnology – Methodology. | LCSH: Ethnology – Research. |
    LCSH: Sociology.
Classification: LCC GN345 .S65 2022 | DDC 305.8001–dc23

We wish to acknowledge the land on which the University of Toronto Press
operates. This land is the traditional territory of the Wendat, the Anishnaabeg,
the Haudenosaunee, the Métis, and the Mississaugas of the Credit First Nation.

This book has been published with the help of a grant from the Federation
for the Humanities and Social Sciences, through the Awards to Scholarly
Publications Program, using funds provided by the Social Sciences and
Humanities Research Council of Canada.

University of Toronto Press acknowledges the financial assistance to its
publishing program of the Canada Council for the Arts and the Ontario Arts
Council, an agency of the Government of Ontario.

Canada Council   Conseil des Arts
for the Arts   du Canada

ONTARIO ARTS COUNCIL
CONSEIL DES ARTS DE L'ONTARIO
an Ontario government agency
un organisme du gouvernement de l'Ontario

Funded by the   Financé par le
Government   gouvernement
of Canada   du Canada

For Harvey

Contents

Part Four: Conclusion

Figures

Acknowledgments

Deep honour and appreciation are owed to Alison's husband, Harvey Swanson, whose extraordinary care and support enabled Alison to play her part in the making of this book in the last difficult years of her life. And we are finally acknowledging just how important Stephan Dobson's wonderful editorial work has been to us, not just for this book but all the way through.

Preface

This is a book about institutional ethnography (IE). It works through and expresses what we, Alison and Dorothy, have learned during our long lives as institutional ethnographers. We were part of its beginning, and of its making and we have learned from doing our own research and teaching. We have both done a lot of graduate student teaching as well as doctoral supervision – you surely learn a great deal working with the unique minds you encounter in the doctoral dialogue. We have also learned, of course, from the work of other institutional ethnographers, who have been wonderfully inventive in opening up the possibilities of a sociology that did not have a history before we went to work in its making. Discovery in researching and writing is what institutional ethnography is up to and we have built this book on the basis of what we have learned from our own researches and thinking as well as from the discoveries made by other institutional ethnographers.

We had been companions in our work as well as good friends for many years. We did not know exactly how our book would take shape; we made sketches of the direction our dialogue might go in, but as the institutional ethnography emerging in our interchange brought aspects into view for us we could not have anticipated, we changed it as we went along. We were also disciplined by having to reread the work of those whose work we were describing. When describing just how colleagues' studies and explorations are, you cannot rely on your selective reading experiences. You have to rediscover their work if you are to accurately describe it. Our book-writing conversation became a new and ongoing experience for us, of discovering together what we had learned in the course of our research and writing but also what we were learning in the actual making of the book. We brought the various topics, strands, themes, and problems together in a dialogue between us in which we were opening up what went beyond what we thought we knew.

Thus writing the book together in email conversations as well as in our occasional opportunities for talk was a process in which we not only learned from each other but learned about aspects of institutional ethnography that were new to us. We made discoveries. We came to see, for example, how the researcher's own life experiences and problems shaped the direction of their research; we made this a specific topic in chapter 8, in which we describe three notable examples of research that were directed by issues and problems in the researchers' lives.

The making of this book was further advanced by the wonderful thoughtfulness and care of those who reviewed it for the publisher. That they were mostly favourable was nice, but of much greater value were thoughtful suggestions for improvement. A couple of the reviewers suggested that we should say something about who our intended readers were. I, Dorothy, writing here (Alison died in September 2019. A draft of the book was complete but Dorothy wrote this preface and made corrections) and speaking for myself, am clear that we did not have definite audiences in mind. However, my sense is that the book's direction and the working out of its writing has been particularly attentive to our experiences as teachers of graduate students and particularly those whose dissertations we supervised (I have supervised to successful conclusion more than forty doctorates). I am also aware of a problem for doctoral students, particularly in the United States, who become fascinated with institutional ethnography but have no professors in their departments who are familiar with the field. Our book was not consciously directed towards audiences of graduate students, but in what we developed I think it likely that our experiences as teachers and advisors in this area were significant in how our book has become what it is. But we certainly did not exclude a more general audience of institutional ethnographers. Institutional ethnographers are always learning.

Institutional ethnography is a sociology that takes up a stance in people's experience in the local sites of their bodily being and seeks to discover what can't be grasped from within that experience, namely the social relations that are implicit in its organization. It calls on sociologists to discover just how the everyday/everynight worlds we participate in are being put together in people's local activities, including, of course, our own. It conceives of the social as actually happening among people who are situated in particular places at particular times, and not as "meaning" or "norms." It draws on people's own good knowledge of their everyday/everynight worlds and does not substitute the expert's "reality" for what people know in their experience. The aim is to create a sociology *for* rather than *of* people that can expand the scope of our knowledge of what we are part of but cannot apprehend directly.

Investigating develops from within the local worlds of people's everyday experience, exploring the social relations and organization that coordinate people's activities across local sites, and explicating the workings of powers that are deeply implicated in our everyday lives. Just how ethnography can be extended into the reaches of institutions, corporations, government, and other forms of organization beyond the local will be developed in the first and second sections of the book. In Part I, we introduce more thoroughly the ontological grounding of this sociology and then, in Part II, we put in place some useful concepts for organizing what to go after in learning from actual people's experience.

In Part III of the book we dig into what is to be learned from the researches of institutional ethnographers. It begins with accounts of how institutional ethnographers have developed effective ways of establishing a research direction into regions that are complex and intersecting. Then we introduce you to some of what has been discovered, of how, when texts are brought into play, they can be seen as what we call "institutional circuits" that bind the local particularities of what's actually getting done by actual people into the abstract generalizing schemata of the authorizing (or boss) texts. Finally we provide an all too brief account of some of the institutional ethnographic work that has been done working with activist projects with a view to making change. This is an aspect of institutional ethnography that was integral to its beginnings in the women's movement in Canada in the mid-1970s.

PART ONE

Introducing Institutional Ethnography

Chapter One

Introduction

But what is institutional ethnography? In its early days as a sociology associated with the women's movement, it got parked in the general category of qualitative sociology. That was a difficulty for us. In a sense, categorizing institutional ethnography as a methodology implied that it could be used in research using standard sociological practices. But it is not a qualitative method; it is more than that. It is a sociology, a method of inquiry into the social that begins and always stays with actual people and their doings; it seeks to discover just how actual people's doings are coordinated with others so that what we might call the ongoing social organizing of our everyday lives actually happens.

Where Institutional Ethnography Got Started

Institutional ethnography originated in Dorothy's search for a "feminist research strategy." In the 1970s, Dorothy set up a women's research centre in Vancouver. It was deliberately dissociated from the University of British Columbia (she was a professor in the Anthropology/Sociology department) and aimed to develop research to support activists in the women's movement emerging at the time. Graduate students working with Dorothy, including Alison, joined in. As we sought to be useful to activists, we came to see that the sociology we had all been trained to work in just didn't do it; it didn't take up exploration from where the women were in their everyday lives and what they were actually confronting and trying to get changed. At a meeting with what had become the Women's Research Centre to discuss possible ways we could be useful, a member of a group of union women told us, "The problem with you sociologists, is that you always end up studying us." This gave force to what was already becoming apparent to Dorothy: a new sociology was needed in which women, and indeed human beings in general, would not be *objects* of study, but *subjects*. A sociology had to be invented in which people would become the subjects; it would be a sociology capable of making visible to people how and where their own lives and doings were caught up in ruling relations extending beyond their own experience and understanding.

Some time before her move to set up a women's research centre, Dorothy had been involved in the Canadianization movement in sociology and had become aware that teaching the sociology she had learned in doing her doctorate at the University of California at Berkeley was a form of intellectual colonialism. Searching for alternatives, she turned to reading Marx and Engels's *The German Ideology* and discovered an alternative way of thinking that would bring her back to where she was working and teaching. Marx and Engels had been redesigning their social science back there in the mid-nineteenth century. Here is the passage that offered Dorothy a different foundation for a social science than the one she had been trained in:

> The premises from which we begin are not arbitrary ones, not dogmas, but real premises from which abstraction can only be made in the imagination. They are the real individuals, their activity and the material conditions under which they live, both those which they find already existing and those produced by their activity. These premises can thus be verified in a purely empirical way. (Marx and Engels, 1973, 36–7)

The original collection of the texts assembled as *The German Ideology* was not published as such in Marx and Engels's lifetime though Engels put together and published an edited version of the first chapters (Marx and Engels, 1973). In the collection as a whole, Marx and Engels were examining the social scientific thinking of those they identified as German ideologists whose social scientific thinking they critically explored in the eight-hundred-some pages of the then unpublished collection. Dorothy read it all. A simple example of their critique begins, "First of all, an abstraction is made from a fact; then it is declared that the fact is based upon the abstraction" (Marx and Engels, 1976, p. 473)." That move is a standard sociological practice: qualitative methods in sociology, for example, are systematized procedures for building generalized abstractions out of the particularizing accounts that describe what's actually going on with people.

Drawing on Marx and Engels's analysis, Dorothy came to see how sociology's conceptual practices displaced people and their actualities. That understanding came together for her with her experience with the Women's Research Centre. A new sociology was needed, grounded in people's actualities, but also with people as subjects rather than as the objects of study.

Inventing a New Sociology

Institutional ethnography's switch to always working with actual people and how what they do coordinates with others is deeply at odds with established sociologies. While there are many approaches, what established sociologies have in common is objectifying language practices that displace people's actions and what is going on among them with concepts. Here is an example from W.R. Scott's work on institutions and organizations (1995).

> Schools receive legitimacy in a society to the extent that their goals are connected to wider cultural values. such as socialization and education, and to the extent that they conform in their structures and procedures to established "patterns of operation" specified for educational organizations. (Scott, 1995, p. xi)

Here we see "schools" and not people receiving legitimacy, whatever that is. And it just arrives; no visible agents transmit it. The abstractions "socialization" and "education" are further abstracted as "wider cultural values" that comfortably play the role of agents, giving legitimacy to schools or taking it away. Once schools have been elevated to the level of generalized abstractions, attributes such as "structures and procedures" can be ascribed to them, enabling them to be evaluated by how they conform to patterns of operation "specified for educational organizations" – though we are never told how and where and by whom such specifications have been made. Constructing discursive entities, "socialization" or "structures," for example, produces a wholly abstract conceptual space in which they can be related to one another as subjects or objects of action without once referring to people or what people actually do.

Institutional ethnographies, by contrast, remain always with actual people and what they do. They might, indeed, be considered an ethology (the study of animal behaviour). Their grounding focus is always in learning from actual people in their everyday lives and how what they do *coordinates* with the actions of others – how we are *social*. The social dimension emerges only as people's actions/activities are taken up as they coordinate them with others. It is never accorded an independent organizational capacity, such as, for example, the way in which the concept of social structure is assigned agency in standard sociological accounts. In this respect, institutional ethnography diverges consciously from sociologies, which have adopted practices in language that displace the presence of people. The constitutive conventions of the language practices of established sociologies remorselessly undermine our attempts to write a sociology from a standpoint in actual people's lives and doings. Michael Billig's critique of the language practices of the social sciences contributes his observations of how verbs locating people's doings get translated into "nominals" that displace the presence of people as agents:

> By rolling out the big nouns, social scientists can avoid describing people and their actions. They can then write in highly unpopulated ways, that is, in ways that do not include people, creating fictional worlds in which their theoretical things, rather than actual people, appear as the major actors. (Billig, 2013, p. 7)

Here's an example from an article in the journal *Organization Studies* of a sentence packed with nominalizations: "CCO [The communicative constituent of organization] scholarship presents communication as the main force that creates, generates, and sustains – *constitutes* – what we consider to be organization and organizing practices" (Schoeneborn et al., 2019, 477). Very striking here is how a nominal "communication" implicitly grounded in people's doings becomes an active "force" and gets things done. People have disappeared.

Though our academic habitus may mean that we use more nominals than we should, institutional ethnographers always stay with actual people's doings. The ongoing discourse of institutional ethnography builds on what we learn from actual people, people who may also be ourselves. But although we learn by listening or watching or both, we are also bringing what we are learning into a dialogue with our prospective ethnography, which has to be built with what we learned. Though we may be, and often are, learning what we had not known was there to be learned, we are at the same time engaging in a dialogue that brings people's telling of what they know in and through their experience into the ethnography lying in wait for us at the next moment of our project. In what we as researchers learn from them about their experiences, or by watching what they do, or in our own participation, we enter into a dialogue with and within the discourse.

The notion of a "dialogue" means something like a conversation. As with text–reader conversations, this dialogue does not require face-to-face interaction. This discursive dialogue is always connected to and organized by ways of thinking, imaging, speaking, writing, seeing, and paying attention to what's going on. We do not own it; we share it with others. In a discursive dialogue, we become active in a complex of relations beyond us, not controlled by us, and yet we are engaged in it. When institutional ethnographers are in this kind of discursive dialogue with the people they are learning from, what is being learned may push them to look beyond established ways of researching and writing towards innovations needed to express what they're discovering.

Doing Ethnography and Discovering Ruling Relations

How then to go about developing an institutional ethnography? What do we look for? What do we write into our notes, locate in texts, track in interviews, or mark up in the transcriptions? When we are just out there as people connecting with other people, as indeed we are when we do fieldwork, there's nothing that tells us what we should be looking for, attending to, noting, questioning in our immediate engagement in the local world we share with others. Something is needed to focus our ethnographic work. And we need to recognize when we are making discoveries.

There is more to institutional ethnography than a focus on what people are actually doing in concert with others. There is more to be looked for. We have suggested the analogy with ethology. So think of an ethologist, Jane Goodall, for example, who is patiently, carefully watching chimpanzees in a national park in Tanzania; she does her observational work by looking, listening, following, even interacting, but what she's after is always as it is for or becomes present to her senses. But the world of people's actions that institutional ethnography takes on has dimensions of actual people's coordinated doings that reach beyond people's sensory scope. The everyday of our lives is organized by what we have come to call *ruling relations* – relations that, though we participate in them, impose their objectified modes upon us.

Contrast the work of the ethologist briefly described above with Janet Rankin and Marie Campbell's book on *Managing to Nurse* (2006), which brings into view some of the ruling relations that shape our experience of a given moment but which originate elsewhere and elsewhen. Their book opens with a description of nurses coming on shift at a hospital:

It is 7:30 a.m., and outside the hospital, the sky is still dark. Nurses arrive at hospital wards for the day shift, most of them wearing pastel pantsuits and athletic shoes. Each wears a name tag that identifies her or his status as Registered Nurse or Licensed Practical Nurse. On Ward A the day nurses gather at the Nursing Station, check a printout of assignments posted on the wall, pick up paper and pencils, and go into the meeting room behind the desk. Listening to a tape-recorded message, they are getting the "shift-change report." One floor below, on Ward B, the change-over routine is slightly different. The newly arrived nurses check a written report left by the night staff, a tick-sheet that summarizes the night-time condition of their patients – their sleep, pain, confusion, incontinence, IV management, and so on – and they make notes, before heading out to begin their work with patients. This is the way an ordinary day begins for these nurses who are taking up their routine tasks as proficient members of a health care team. (Rankin and Campbell, 2006, p. 4)

What is described here is pretty much what we might be able to observe if we rose early enough to be present as the morning shift comes on in any hospital in Canada. But looking carefully at the words used in this description, we can recognize a complex of generalizing relations that are implicit in it. Though we may hardly notice, there are words locating such relations, present and taken for granted and yet not actually observable, that are integral to the description. Using the same passage, I've marked these words in bold italics:

It is 7:30 a.m., and outside the *hospital*, the sky is still dark. *Nurses* arrive at *hospital wards* for the *day shift*, most of them wearing pastel pantsuits and athletic shoes. Each wears a name tag that identifies her or his status as *Registered Nurse* or *Licensed Practical Nurse*. On *Ward A* the day nurses gather at the *Nursing Station*, check a printout of *assignments* posted on the wall, pick up paper and pencils, and go into the meeting room behind the desk. Listening to a tape-recorded message, they are getting the '*shift-change report.*' One floor below, on *Ward B*, the *change-over* routine is slightly different. The newly arrived *nurses* check a written report left by the *night staff*, a *tick-sheet* that summarizes the night-time condition of their patients – *their sleep, pain, confusion, incontinence, IV management, and so on* – and they make notes, before heading out to begin their work with patients. This is the way an ordinary day begins for these *nurses* who are taking up their routine tasks as proficient members of a *health care team*. (Rankin and Campbell, 2006, p. 4)

The marked words locate the embedding of this daily local practice in relations that are not discoverable or observable in that place, at that time, and among those people. A "hospital," for example, is more than just the building the nurses are entering to do their work. It only exists as a hospital as the established workplace where legally certified professionals provide care and remedy to people needing them. In Canada, it will be connected up organizationally, managerially, and financially with the provincial health care system. You may be able to pick out other terms that hook up with one another in such relations. Categories such as "Registered Nurse" and "Licensed Practical Nurse" carry implicit references to other institutional complexes such as colleges or universities with programs of training required for someone to be "certified" as of this status. There are implications here of job-market relations and of the role of the medical profession in the certification of nurses. Here we can begin to see what we are talking about when we use terms such as "institutional" or "institution" – the complex of relations that are present, but not actually observed or observable in the physical setting in the same way as the dark sky, the wall, the paper, and pencils can be seen and felt. The relations organizing what people are doing there in the hospital are standardized and generalized across local settings via texts, but also in the habits, training, and traditions that the nurses carry with them, their skills, their professional and technical discourse that generalize again across multiple local settings and enable their distinctive work to complement that of other professionals – in this case, in the hospital setting. When Marx and Engels were developing their social science grounded in real people and the realities of the activities and conditions of their lives, they also wrote what we might call their *problematic* by introducing for exploration relations existing in some sense independently of particular people. They wrote:

> Individuals always started, and always start, from themselves. Their relations are the relations of their real life. How does it happen that their relations assume an independent existence over against them? And that the forces of their own life overpower them? (Marx and Engels, 1973, p. 14)

For Marx and Engels, the relations assuming an independent existence over and against individuals were those organized in monetary exchanges, a form of abstraction that displaces the presence of individuals as individuals while existing only in what people actually do. What people do in the very ordinary ways of our lives is organized by complexes of relations that extend beyond us, for example in the monetary exchanges referred to above. The objectifying relations of ruling that engage the exploration of institutional ethnography are those in which the sequences of action are coordinated by replicable texts that can be read or seen or heard in more than one place at more than one time and by more than one person. Though money is a form of text, the texts that preoccupy institutional ethnography are those in words (numbers may be included). Though we always start with ourselves, are always in our bodily being and hence located in our everyday worlds, our doings/ our work are coordinated translocally with the doings/work of others through the text-mediated ruling relations. And thus we participate in and empower relations that stand over against us and overpower our lives. This is the focus of institutional ethnography's exploration.

The Book

This first chapter of this book lays out the basics of how institutional ethnography proceeds as a sociology that does not call for theory and is not in the business of explaining human social behaviour. The connection has been made to Marx and Engels's crucial shift in thinking to a social science grounded in actual people, their work, and the real conditions of their lives. This is where institutional ethnography does its investigating, opening up and discovering how what people are actually doing is caught up in and coordinated in institutional relations that reach beyond them and overpower their lives. Chapter 2, which provides an introduction to Part II, presents the notion of developing an ethnography as a sequence of two dialogues: the first is when the researcher engages with people who become her or his source of knowledge about how things are getting done and about who is doing what. S/he learns from their experience; but experience is always a dialogue, and though the ethnographer's commitment is to remaining open to what can be learned from those s/he works with as informants, and although s/he, hopefully, will learn something s/he did not even know s/he might expect, at the same time she has an interest; there will be topics she wants to open up. That's what we mean as the first dialogue. The second is when there is data and the ethnographer is figuring out what she is discovering or has discovered that can be written as an ethnography.

The four chapters of Part II then introduce concepts that institutional ethnographers have found useful in organizing their first dialogue, making sure that whatever else they learn, these general areas do not get left out. Though in a sense this is theory, the concepts of "discourse," "work," and "text" aren't intended to impose interpretation or a selective frame. They are meant, rather, to suggest the ethnographer's attention to what may be drawn from people's experiential knowledge that will be useful in developing an ethnography. The term "discourse" draws on Michel Foucault, but turns the direction of interest towards institutional language practices that the researcher may or may not be familiar with. It happens sometimes that the researcher is a knowledgeable participant of the same discourse as the informants s/he's talking to, and may miss out on the concrete detail of what they do and how they coordinate with others because the researcher assumes s/he knows what the informant is talking about – but it isn't to be found in the transcribed interview.

Chapter 5 is about work and introduces the idea of thinking of work much beyond our standard ways and close to notions of work evolving in the women's movement – as women's work, as housewives and mothers, came to be recognized as work. The notion of "work" here extends to what people do and mean to do and that takes time and effort. When Dorothy sits in the summer backyard in the evening waiting for the bachelor crows to fly from their local homes to an assembly in a park of large trees in Burnaby, on nearby buildings, and on the telephone wires, she is working. She means to be there; she arranges her body to be comfortable waiting in her canvas chair to watch the crows fly; she attends to the fading of the sun which signals the crows to take off and she means to do it. This generous conception of work is very useful in exploring with informants just how things are actually getting done.

The final concept suggested for data collection is the notion of "text," the subject of chapter 6. Texts, particularly texts that are replicated and available to more than one person and at different times, are essential to the very existence of what we are calling institutional or ruling relations. Chapter 6 makes clear that texts are never to be taken up as in and for themselves or in relation to other texts, but are always and only brought into research focus as they enter into and coordinate what people are actually doing. These are the essential coordinators of what people do at the level of ruling relations, and discovering what people are doing that involves texts, either directly or indirectly, is essential to developing an institutional ethnography.

Then in Part III, a second dialogue is brought into view – the researcher's shift from what is being or has been learned from individuals to building an ethnography that makes visible how what has been learned from respondents can be seen and shown as coordinated sequences of social relations that reach beyond the particularities of people's local experience of what they do. In chapter 9, the work of notable institutional ethnographers George Smith, Gerald de Montigny, Janet Rankin, and Marie Campbell is described in some detail in order to show how the problematic of their concerns and interests, arising in their own lives, entered into and organized the direction of their ethnographies. Chapter 10 moves to an account of some of what has been discovered about how ruling texts organize the representations of the local particularities of people's doings, with a special focus on "institutional circuits." It describes research specifically oriented to making change from below, drawing mainly on the work of Ellen Pence on the judicial processing of domestic abuse in Duluth, Minnesota, and of Susan Turner, with her associates Julie Bomberry and Amye Werner, on the policing of sexual violence on the Six Nations Reserve in Ontario. The final chapter draws together Alison's and Dorothy's reflections on what we have learned in the making of this book and on what we see as having been built as a basis on which institutional ethnography may go forward.

Chapter Two

People's Experience as the Ethnographic Resource

By taking up a research problematic grounded in people's everyday lives as they know and experience them, institutional ethnography is designing and developing an alternate sociology. It learns from and relies on people's experience of the actualities of their lives and doings. Marie Campbell emphasizes it is "the conceptual framing of everyday experience heard or read about or observed [that] constitutes one of the distinctive features of institutional ethnography" (Campbell, 2006, p. 92). The grounding of the ethnography is always the actual practices of actual individuals as they go forward in actual settings and at actual times in coordination with others. At the same time, the research reaches beyond what individuals know and experience to discover how the social relations extending beyond individuals and beyond the everyday enter into and organize our lives. These are relations integral to our everyday lives and may be very much taken for granted. For example, in Dorothy and Alison's study of the work mothers do in relation to their children's schooling (described more fully below) we took up how the legally grounded organization of the school day dominated the work of their weekday lives. Inquiry may also expand into social relations extending beyond individuals to learn about someone's actions as a "moment" in a sequence in which others have been or will be acting. This "moment" is situated in the ongoing, concerting, and coordinating of individuals' activities. Here is the social as the discursively constituted object of IE's business. *In any particular ethnographic project, it is to be discovered, not theorized.* The researcher learns from people's own experience of their doings as they tell it, or from observation, or from a combination of the two. Hence, for institutional ethnographers, those the researcher works with are not the objects of study; they are the subjects of study. We have to *learn from* people about what they do and how they go about it.

Dorothy interpolates at this point that she has just finished a careful description in an email of how she made a very delicious sauce to go with cooked chicken thighs to be served on polenta. She had no recipe, but flavoured it up as she went along, and luckily it turned out very well indeed. She reports that she could add more detail to her description because the process of describing evoked what she actually did. As with the recipe, in an institutional ethnography there is always more to say. The ethnographer's interviews – or perhaps better, "conversations" – with respondents are analogous. IE interviews draw on people's experience of what they do because they are active in those relations that are the focus of the researcher's inquiry. Ethnographers may also draw on less formalized conversations. In any case, we are learning from what people know from their experience. We build an ethnography by assembling and exploring the organization of relations in which those we've learned from are active. We build what might be described as a map of the relations that extend beyond what the informants we have learned from can see from where they are situated in the social world. Thus, IE research assembles people's experiential knowledge from selected and articulated sites. Instead of starting with theories or concepts, as is standard sociological procedure, institutional ethnography stays always with actual individuals in their bodily being, with their doings, and with how what they are doing coordinates with others' activities. This means that rather than observing or interviewing in traditional sociological fashion, the institutional ethnographer is *learning from* those with whom s/he engages in a work of discovery that goes beyond what any one individual knows.

Alison and Dorothy were both single parents with sons in elementary school when we started working together. Alison's dissertation focused on the educational stereotyping of "single parents," exploring how the concept came into play in schools and in administrative contexts in Toronto. We used to get together and bitch about how we were treated as "defective" parents, and eventually came together to develop a research project that would create an understanding of why "single parents" were such a problem for schools. We undertook research that would seek to learn about the work some mothers were doing that actively contributed to work getting done in their children's schools and the implications for schools if mothers did not have time or were otherwise not able to make that contribution. We eventually wrote a book on mothering work (Griffith and Smith, 2005). We had interviewed mothers who worked inside the family home and mothers who were engaged in paid work. As the mothers spoke of their everyday mothering work, it became clear to us that their work was coordinated with the daily routines of the school (e.g., getting children up and off to school "on time"). But there was more going on than simply mothers' work and school routines. What does it mean to be "on time" for school? Who decides what that time is? In order to answer these ordinary questions, we had to look towards the policies generated at the level of the school boards and further, towards the Ontario Education Act, which dictates the number of educational hours that constitute a school year. In this research example, the mothers' actual everyday work is coordinated with the texts of public schooling and hence, of course, also with how teachers' school-day schedules connect to class start time. We learned in talking with school principals that even a few late arrivals can disorganize the start of a class. The map of relations that began in mothering work extends beyond the particular household.

Recently, at the time of writing, there was some talk on CBC radio about the "mental work" that women do in the household. This kind of work is characterized as all those often-invisible household and childcare and emotional tasks that women do. Our research on mothering (Griffith and Smith, 2005) and DeVault's ethnographic work on "feeding the family" (1991) takes this interesting but superficial descriptive analysis one step further. We did not just discover these, often invisible, tasks, but asked what the institutional relations are that coordinate them as gendered work in which the everyday family routines are linked with school routines such as getting to school on time or doing the weekly shopping that ensures that family members' different food preferences are attended to. And so on. Behind the everyday of women's work coordinating the family lie the institutional relations of schooling, the corporate relations of food production and marketing, and so on.

The ethnographic research work of institutional ethnography is always with actual people whose everyday lives and doings are caught up in relations that extend beyond what can be observed from within their experience. Whether using observation or relying largely on talking with people to learn from them, the work of research is essentially a dialogue. What is observed or what the researcher is learning from interviews is always, on the researcher's part, a hybrid conversation knitting the ongoing conversation with a respondent (or observation of people's work) with institutional ethnographic discourse. We may be talking with someone and hearing of their experiences, but then there is always this invisible other, the ethnography to be written to be read by others. There are, in a sense, two dialogues or two stages of dialogue. One is when we learn from those we are speaking to and learning from or observing; the other is when we are bringing together what we have learned to create the ethnographic account for our readers.

We want to make clear that when we introduce the notion of two stages of dialogue or two dialogues, we are not suggesting methodological sequencing, "collecting" what becomes "data," which is then followed by "data analysis." An institutional ethnography is a work of discovery throughout the research process. We begin to be able to see how things are being put together during our first dialogue with informants. Reviewing that data in the process of discovery then points to new directions or suggests building further dialogues with those active in whatever sequence we begin to discover. From what we have learned at one moment in the research, we can see more that needs to be known – where our further explorations should go and who we should be talking to and what we need to learn. The ethnography is built up as we go along, becoming, of course, clearer and more explicit at the time of actually writing the ethnography (more about this in chapter 7). Writing itself is a dialogue between what we are trying to say and the discourse/s in which we are participating. It is itself also a source of discoveries that reflect on and can open up further aspects of our research dialogues that we had not been aware of before. In a sense, an institutional ethnography, like all research, is never finished. More can always be said. The notions of first and second dialogues are not intended as a methodological guide, but simply as a way of drawing attention to the different ways our interests and intentions are organized, first at the stage of basic learning from people's experience and then how to travel from what we've learned to what we have to tell.

Institutional ethnography has been growing and developing largely through research. As we, the authors, in the course of writing, have been talking, emailing each other, and thinking, we have been in dialogue with the research and thinking of other institutional ethnographers (as well as with our own). Of course, any such moment is already outdated; we are learning all the time from others' research and from conversations at conferences, in our homes, or perhaps over coffee or during meals. Innovations in IE come as researchers discover problems in their encounter with people's actualities that have not been encountered before in previous IE research. Working concepts that have proved useful in the ethnographic dialogue have emerged as people have wrestled with the problem of discovering everyday worlds that just do not fit the established discursive conceptual practices. Something has to be invented, and it has been methods discovered in the course of creating an ethnography in a specific institutional region that then contribute resources that others can draw on. We are thinking here, for example, of Susan Turner's innovative strategies for mapping text–work–text sequences (Turner 2001, 2003) which will be a topic in our chapter on "texts" (chapter 6). We are, after all, exploring the same chain of mountains; we are discovering together how the ruling relations are being put together and how they organize our everyday lives.

In connecting institutional ethnography research with actual situations and people, the ethnographer is learning. Ignorance is a strength, because it orients the researcher's hybrid dialogues with those from whom we're learning. The term "hybrid" draws on Mikhail Bakhtin's (1981) account of utterances that incorporate more than one speaker, whether as quotes or as an implicit second presence. In an ethnographic interview, the researcher's engagement in the unspoken discursive dialogue is for the most part implicit. At the interface between the everyday actualities of the researcher's work and what those s/he is working with are doing, dialogue is hybrid. The researcher is observing, or asking questions, or simply listening – her/his posture, eye focus, "ums" and "ahs" express listening to the respondent. The researcher does not yet know just what s/he has to find out, but concepts and methods built up in the IE discourse give direction. Additionally, there is implicit in this dialogue a secondary dialogue relating the researcher's local conversations with respondents to the community of knowledgeable readers for whom the researcher will be writing the ethnography.

As stressed above, doing institutional ethnographic research draws on people's experience. This ensures that the subject's understandings and viewpoints are preserved in what becomes "data" for the purposes of writing the ethnography. The word "experience" reminds us that the researcher is always learning about how things are put together from the perspective of the respondent; what s/he has to tell may include feelings, but the telling must always get down to what is or was done and was happening – including language, thinking, and feeling.

The interview dialogue, therefore, should orient the interview or talk to the *concrete* of what the respondent *knows* about his or her doings, how they get things done, the words they use. Here is where the dialogue engages; the ethnographer needs to learn the concrete of what the respondent experiences and encourages the respondent to come down from institutional abstractions, such as the teacher's use of the term "levels" in talking about her or his classroom work. The ethnographer wants to know more, wants to know what s/he is talking about, and asks for examples or descriptions.

The term "experience" may be deceptive, since it seems to be referring to what it was like for the teller when something was actually happening or going on. But it is important to recognize that when someone is speaking from their experience it is essentially a dialogue (e.g., Mishler, 1986). S/he is drawing selectively on memory and bringing it into relevance for the hearer. An interview drawing on an experiential account of someone's work, for example, is organized dialogically, in talk. Dorothy's description (above) of writing up how she made a sauce for supper draws on her experience to spell out how it might be possible to make the dish again. More must have been going on at the time she was actually making the dish, but she picked out only those aspects relevant to a remake.

So in an interview with a respondent, the institutional ethnographer draws on the respondent's experience – in a sense, helps to create it as memory gets organized in the telling. But the dialogue with the respondent is also a dialogue with the researcher's IE project. Thus someone's experience as an ethnographic resource spoken to the researcher has to be organized by the researcher, yet without dominating and imposing pre-set interpretations. The researcher must be open to being changed, to finding that what had been thought at the outset of the research is turning out to be very different. Learning has a direction, but it is also following what is new and had not been known in advance. In a sense, the researcher acts as a bridge between the respondent who draws on memory in telling about their experience and institutional ethnographic discourse. The researcher is not interested, for example, in getting wholly accurate accounts of some particular event, but rather in the respondent's knowledge of how something was done and then how it was connected up with sequences of action beyond the individual. As we shall see in chapter 10, when police on the Six Nations Reserve respond to a complaint of sexual violence, they go to work in ways that will connect what they find to the legal/judicial institutions of Ontario reaching beyond the reserve. Learning from the experience of those the researcher engages with always has this possibility of reaching further into what the respondent can remember of particular situations and events. The researcher wants concrete accounts, detail, and elaboration since the more s/he learns, the better s/he is able to recognize how what the respondent is telling her or him is hooked up into relations beyond a particular description. Experiential dialogue can always explore back to what the respondent has known or knows directly and the concrete and specific is always of major importance in grounding the ethnographer's data.

When Dorothy was in the early stages of working on this book, she read a volume of collected materials assembled by Pierre Bourdieu (Bourdieu et al., 1999) drawing on the experiences of people living in marginalized situations, as told in interviews with social scientists (including Bourdieu). The project brought together the interviews with various chapters by social scientists and was designed by Bourdieu to make visible the actual situations of real people suffering under an economic and political regime that had become incapable of recognizing or responding to their realities. The aim of the project as social science was to make the actual situations of marginalized people visible. Participants were chosen to represent different social categories, a teacher, a shopkeeper, and so on, and as located in impoverished communities or projects. In his introduction, Bourdieu writes as follows to the reader in his preface,

> "Do not deplore, do not laugh, do not hate – understand." There is no point in sociologists adopting Spinoza's precept if they are unable to put it into practice. But how can we offer readers the means of understanding – which means taking people as they are – except by providing the theoretical instruments that let us see these lives as necessary through a systematic search for the causes and reasons they have for being what they are? ... The analyst's intrusion is as difficult as it is necessary. It must proclaim itself openly and yet strive to go unnoticed. These considerations led us to present the cases so that the reading connects individuals whose completely different points of view might very well be at odds, even clash, in real life. This order also allows us to highlight the representative nature of each case, whether it is a teacher or shopkeeper or whoever, by grouping it with other 'cases' that are, so to speak, variants of it. (Bourdieu et al., 1999, p. 1)

Bourdieu's project, as worked through with other social scientists, opens up and explores how particular individuals living in marginalized conditions experience and respond to their situations. The interviews are rich and telling. But what this approach might have in common with institutional ethnography concludes there. In the Bourdieu et al. collection, each subject tells her or his own distinctive story, but learning from the individual accounts is pre-empted by analysis that shows how it is to be treated as representative of a given social category – craftsman, teacher, shopkeeper, and so on. In institutional ethnography, we move from people's telling of their experiences and from their knowledge of their own doings to exploring the ruling relations that enter into and overpower their lives.

Institutional ethnography, therefore, works with inquiry and discovery. The aim in institutional ethnography is not to find in an individual's experience what can be learned about members of a given social category in general. People remain subjects; they do not become objects. Ethnographic inquiry engages the researcher in a dialogue with people's actualities as they experience them and as they are organized by relations extending beyond any one person's experience. Hence, inquiry in institutional ethnography is always a dialogue in which the researcher – and through her or him, the discourse – is being changed. Institutional ethnographers learn from people's own experience, their knowledge of what they do and participate in; the ethnographer builds upon this by learning from other people whose work is coordinated with theirs in the objectified and objectifying ruling relations. Institutional ethnography is more like cartography than explanation: though the ethnographer connects with people with an orientation and interest shaped by IE discourse, s/he does not impose an interpretation drawn from theory, but builds what has been learned from watching, from interviews, and from taking up the textual mediations of the ruling relations as organized activities in people's local lives. It is a complex of dialogues.

This ethnographic dialogue relies on people's doings, not as events, but as people's knowledge of how they get things done. It relies on the social as something that happens among people and therefore is never identifiable with what one individual does and knows how to do. It takes for granted that there will be more than one way of being active and more than one perspective on an individual's own and other activities. As a participant, the informant will be able to describe how she gets things done in her work. The ethnographer in the course of her or his research aims to find out how things are connected up, particularly by focusing on how language both organizes and often makes invisible the very concerting of people's activities that the ethnographer wants to find.

Of course, the ethnographer's dialogue with those she wants to learn from does not lack direction. When Dorothy went out as an innocent graduate student simply to observe, she found that simply observing is disorganizing. It means not knowing how to look, what to select, what to ask, what to follow up, and the problem is only overcome when s/he finds a direction, even though it has not originated in research questions posed before she entered the field. That experience betrays the ordinary problem that our lived world is not already spoken and becomes formless when we try to find form in it, not recognizing that it only comes into being for us in our interplay with one another. If the institutional ethnographer is mapping the social relations and organization in which the people s/he is working with are active, s/he has to have some idea of what s/he is looking at and for, even though what s/he started with may change as s/he learns.

We have thus come to see ethnography as an essentially dialogic method; the ethnographer begins by learning directly from people, talking with them in ordinary ways or in interviews, and/or observing. That is the first or primary dialogue, and it relies deeply on people's experience, *including the ethnographer's*. But ethnographers must also take what they have learned and begin to engage with a second dialogue that develops as the ethnography is being written for participants in the discourse of institutional ethnography. Drawing on what is learned in the double dialogue, the ethnographer can write or speak back to those who are concerned with issues that have emerged. And notice here that the institutional ethnographer does not create data in the sense of factual information that has been established as independent of the original respondents or themselves.

What is striking about people's experiential resources is that they can always tell more. The extent of what becomes knowledge between respondent and researcher can be overwhelming in its extent and richness. The respondent is being recognized in a local practice as someone with expert knowledge to impart to the ignoramus who is doing the interview. When Dorothy was working with Stephan Dobson (Smith and Dobson, 2011) on a study of changes to steelworker training, she had arranged an interview with a steelworker through the union; they met in the union's formal meeting room – an impressive room with a large long table and large chairs. The steelworker respondent was reluctant, perhaps intimidated. He said that he didn't have anything much to tell and was probably only available for a short time. Two hours later, Dorothy was getting exhausted and he was still talking about his job, how he taught other workers how to do it, what and how he had learned when he first started in the mill. He knew so much and had so much to tell that was relevant to what Dorothy needed to know and *was discovering* that she needed to know.

When people speak experientially, they draw on an indefinitely expandable resource of knowledge. And that, mostly, respondents really seem to enjoy the interview process is likely because it gives pleasure to be able to speak freely and with expert knowledge of what, generally, no one is particularly interested in or wants to hear about. For the respondent, here, at last, is a listener, one who wants to learn from you. Of course, Dorothy had the occasional question, probably general ones, when she wanted to hear more or didn't quite understand what the steelworker was talking about, but her interest in how workers learned was a topic of which he had extensive experience, and as he spoke what he said suggested more. Though Dorothy occasionally intervened, she never dictated, never had set questions, never imposed an interpretation. That does not mean, however, that she went in with no knowledge. She had read in the area, she had spoken with others about the upcoming interviews; she may even have had a list of topics she hoped to cover. In listening, she got to know a lot that she had not even anticipated or known she would want to know. Drawing on people's experience in interviews set up to allow the respondent enough time to expand on what s/he knows directly as part of everyday life can be very effective. All of a sudden people discover that there's someone else who's fascinated by the knowledge and skills that they've perhaps never recognized that they had and in which no one has ever expressed a depth of interest comparable to the researcher's.

But the experience that the researcher draws on may also be his or her own. In a sense, of course, doing observation systematizes the researcher's own experiential practices. Particularly useful is drawing out a developed account of the experience or experiences that entered into framing the research problematic, that is, the general direction and focus of inquiry Alison drew on her experiences of being labelled "single parent" to frame the inquiry for her dissertation, discovering in the academic discourse, the administrative organization of public schooling in Toronto, and the discourse of teachers and principals in Toronto public schools the institutional relations organizing the everyday of her and her sons' schooling experience. Her dialogue began before she was a graduate student, speaking with other single parents about the "troubles" their children had in school. There were no answers. As a graduate student, the dialogues expanded to include noting the comments that other students made about the "trouble" with children from single-parent families; the literature on the problems of single-parent families; interviews with teachers, social workers, and administrators about single-parent-families' differences. The research expanded to include stories in the newspapers and school board minutes leading up to policy decisions addressing differences among students. Working with these dialogues meant that Alison was able to speak to the questions asked by single parents about their children's troubles in school. So, too, teachers and administrators were interested to discover the processes through which children from single-parent families became a problem for their school.

Dorothy and Alison shared an interest in mothering work and, as mentioned earlier, both of us were single parents with two sons in public schools. We shared our experiences of being identified as "single parents" in the public school as we went on walks together in the Toronto ravines. Our conversations, as well as Alison's dissertation, led to a project of research that looked at the work mothers do in relation to their children's school and how the background educational work undertaken in the home is actually done and at what level of parental skills (Griffith and Smith, 2005). The work in school of teachers and students is organized to be responsive to work done – or not done – in the home, including, as mentioned earlier, the regularity of the school day. In all such instances in which institutional ethnographers begin with learning about and from people's experiences, their own and/or those of respondents, we can see how inquiry moves from the particularities of actual people's lives to the generalizing institutional relations that overpower them.

Here then, we summarize the main ways in which institutional ethnography diverges from what, perhaps, we could call the mainstream of sociology (which, of course, has many varieties). Here are four main points:

i. Breaking with the centrality of abstract concepts displacing and subsuming accounts of what's actually going on among people;
ii. Moving from making people the objects of study (explaining their behaviour, etc.) to making them the subjects whose everyday experience is an authoritative source for the ethnographer;
iii. Avoiding conceptual or methodological tracks that individualize or attach what we learn to individuals as properties or attributes;
iv. Opening up the work of discovering and mapping for people's use how people are active in the objectified (or ruling) relations that exist independently of us and overpower our lives.

PART TWO

Useful Concepts

Chapter Three

Concepts but Not Theory

We have stressed the essentially dialogic character of ethnographic research. As we have pointed out, there are indeed two moments of dialogue in producing the ethnography as it's finally written, for those who share in institutional ethnographic discourse or for those who need to understand how issues in their lives are hooked into ruling relations. Research begins with the ethnographer's work of learning from actual people about what they do. S/he has to be open to what people have to tell or what comes from what s/he observes. What is being learned is not controlled. At the same time, the ethnographer does engage in a dialogue into which s/he inserts interests relevant to creating an institutional ethnography. S/he may ask the respondent to give concrete examples, or simply to tell more, but s/he may also have specific interests guided by the concepts that will be introduced in the following three chapters. When interviewing, Dorothy and Alison generally encourage the respondent to continue, to tell more, with minor interventions or even moments of silence, which are understood as waiting for more. We may also have very specific questions that are seen as necessary to building the ethnography, but these can wait until the respondent has more or less done their part, and can be inserted at the end so as not to interrupt

Integral to the research is the first moment of engaging with those the ethnographer learns from. Whether by talking with them, observing what they do, or drawing on his or her own experience, or some combination, there is a dialogue in which the researcher is learning. S/he does not know what to expect, what will be learned, and where the respondent may take her or him. It can actually be a special problem to be interviewing someone who works in the same professional area as the ethnographer, who all too easily takes her/his own knowledge for granted. Ignorance is a great advantage in institutional ethnographic research.

The dialogue of learning from people's experience – which may include the ethnographer's own experience – is essential to the ethnography but it is not yet an ethnography. There is a second dialogue, when the ethnographer is drawing on what s/he has learned, to build the ethnography to be presented or published. The second dialogue builds on what has been learned in the first, bringing what has been learned into a written account for those who may read. The first dialogues build what is ordinarily described as the "data." Data is what is already given – that's the Latin origin of the term – and is there to be written into the ethnography. In this context, the term "data" refers to what the ethnographer has learned about people's doings or practices by talking with those involved or observing them. Now they are in some fixed textual form, transcriptions, or audio recordings. As "data," these first dialogues are then drawn into the second moment of dialogue. Coding is to be avoided because it is a procedure that generalizes in a standardizing mode, but if the data is extensive, it may be useful to index the varied content to help the work of building the ethnography. Indexing is fully responsive to the actual content and does not impose a system of categories.

In the previous chapter, we saw that these two dialogues are not wholly separated in practice. In the process of developing her or his representational account, the ethnographer may discover that more needs to be learned in particular areas and, hence, that more research is needed. Overall, the IE project is exploration and discovery. Nonetheless, the two moments of ethnographic dialogue are rather different. In this part of the book, we will be concerned with concepts that are usefully involved because they help to guide the researcher's interests in her or his interchange with respondents or in what s/he should be attending to in making observations. The main topic of Part III of the book is to bring into view some of what institutional ethnographers have developed in creating ethnographies that bring ruling relations into view as people's actual practices.

We have already given some general idea of the institutional ethnographic discourse that is activated in the researcher's dialogue with what s/he observes or learns in conversation with respondents. The most general ordering provided by institutional ethnographic discourse is its grounding in actual people's doings, in their experience, and in how what they do is coordinated with others. And we must remember that language is something people do both out loud and in their heads and is integral to how people's doings are coordinated. Recognizing words as actual practices brings them within ethnographic scope. In a later part of this book, when we turn to describing something of actual research practices, language will become a focus again.

Right here, however, we need to focus on concepts as practices and work out how to use the concepts that institutional ethnographers have found to be helpful in the ethnographic dialogue. Gilbert Ryle, a British "ordinary language" philosopher, writes of concepts as practices and of how they operate; he observes how people do theorizing; for him, theorizing is "an activity ... mostly performed in silence but nonetheless performed" (Ryle, 1949, p. 27). The institutional ethnographic conceptual practices are not theories but they are indeed an activity that is actually performed, though we may not be aware of it as such. This part of the book, Part II, introduces conceptual practices that have been found to be useful in orienting the data collection process and in helping the researcher's focus when engaged in dialogue with respondents.

It is important here to stress again that the concepts institutional ethnographers have found useful to bring into play in their research have no theoretical function. They are not used to interpret or formulate what is being learned from talking with people or observation. When research is dominated by concepts and theories that direct the research selectively, people become no more than sources of material to be interpreted in those terms – they become the objects of research. It is standard practice in qualitative sociology to establish a set of codes that can be applied across the board to all the respondents who have been interviewed. Characteristically, interviews are undertaken using standardized questions, whether or not those interviewed are responsive to them or can even make sense of them. Dorothy remembers being interviewed using formalized questions when she was a student at the University of California, Berkeley, and how, with the researcher's encouragement, she had to answer questions with coded answers, none of which actually fit her situation. The formalized questions were designed to fit whatever the theoretical framework had been, but simply had no answer in her life. But she gave answers. Methods of that kind ensure that analysis of the resulting data will conform to the conceptual frame that the data collection has been designed to fit. Those subjected to the sociologist's conceptual dominance play no part as actual people in making the research findings; they become mere resources for sociological generalization. Such language practices select for attention only those aspects of people's experience of what is going on with them that can be fitted to the concepts and frameworks of the discourse. Theory operates as a "shell" controlling the content by which it can be filled and excluding what does not (more on "shells" in chapter 9 on "textual realities"). Actualities as experienced and fitted to the theoretical shell become no more than instances or examples of the author's generalizing. People as subjects are displaced.

In what follows, the concepts of "discourse," "work," and "texts" introduce, explicate, and elaborate something of how institutional ethnographers have been "performing" them and what they have opened up for us. These are concepts that can bring into focus aspects of people's doings that we might not otherwise be aware of or recognize as coordinating people's doings. We emphasize that their use is not required. They may be found not relevant to exploring with respondents the problems of their lives that the researcher may be developing as his or her problematic. These are, however, concepts that can be very helpful in grounding what becomes our data in people's own knowledge of how they go about things in their everyday life. They help to orient our part in the dialogue so that what we learn will include aspects that are particularly relevant to the institutional ethnography – the second dialogue. They enable discoveries in what the respondent can tell that go beyond what has already been learned. The concepts "discourse," "work," and "texts" have been found to help in organizing and directing dialogic attention without imposing interpretations. They help in ensuring that what we are learning, particularly in interviews, doesn't just wander all over the place – which can easily happen when people get going in the kind of freedom that speaking from their experience creates. Of course we want respondents to be able to speak freely from their experience but at the same time we need to make sure that they include aspects of what they have lived that might go missing in the ordinary process of talking.

The concept of discourse is the first concept we will look at. We do need to be aware of the language people are using to speak their experience. There can be a problem if respondent and ethnographer are both workers in the same institutional profession. The ethnographer may all too easily take for granted that s/he knows what the respondent is talking about when the institutional language is used – but the information will not be there in the transcript when it becomes his or her data. But we may also need to learn something of the discourse the respondent participates in.

The second is what we call institutional ethnography's generous conception of work. Rather than sticking with the ordinary use of the term, which refers primarily to what people are paid to do, this conception of work draws the ethnographer's attention to anything that people may be doing that they mean to do and that takes time and bodily effort. It is a concept that allows us to recognize and attend to people's thinking and feeling as what is being done.

The third draws "texts" into ethnographic focus as a means of bringing institutional forms of organizing within the scope of ethnographic inquiry. "Texts" as the word is used here does not carry theoretical weight. Rather, it draws the researcher's attention to material media that carry messages, images, and sounds, using technologies that displace the presence of whoever made them. Recognizing these ethnographically, that is, as they actually enter into actively coordinating people's doings, has proven essential to developing ethnographies of institutional and organizational relations – the ruling relations that overpower our lives.

Such concepts bring into view aspects of the social world that may be taken for granted. As emphasized here, they are useful for organizing the ethnographer's dialogue with those speaking of their experiences in an interview or simply from what they tell in a conversation with the researcher who is working observationally. We stress that these are concepts organizing the researcher's practices but they are not imposed on those we talk to or even introduced to them. They guide our interest, where we might ask the respondent to tell us more, to give concrete examples and so on. We will, of course, also be learning what we had not expected but we still have these interests that will enter into and modify how we are participating in the first dialogue, the dialogue of learning.

In such talk, people's experiences always emerge as organized in the words in which they are spoken; such talk also always holds the possibility of yielding more concrete detail as the interchange between researcher and respondent continues. A respondent, being interviewed, can dig further into memory and expand on what has drawn the interviewer's interest. When abstractions intervene, as happens rather too readily in sociological interviewing practices, the researcher's own practices of concepts, such as "discourse," "work," and "text," can alert her or him to ask for concrete instances of what the respondent seems to be talking about but has not actually told. In their collaborative studies of what they call work (more on this in chapter 5 on "work"), Eric Mykhalovskiy (2002) and Liza McCoy (2002) emphasize that IE research does not begin with fixed theoretical categories or concepts that an ethnographer uses in selectively collecting and analysing data. In taking up the institutional ethnographic "generous" conception of work to explore the example of people living with AIDS (PHAs) receiving retroviral therapies, Mykhalovskiy and McCoy stress that the concept of work is "empty"; it "guides"; it does not impose categories or interpretations, but it opens doors.

Let us, in conclusion, be clear. Though these are concepts that have proven useful, they are not exclusive nor even required – though it is probably hard to engage with ruling relations ethnographically without paying attention to how such relations are text-coordinated. Let us be clear, also, that these are concepts that help the ethnographer in the research process orient to what may be going on; the three terms, discourse, work, and text, are those that help to organize the researcher's attention as s/he is listening to a respondent speaking from their own everyday knowledge of what they do and are part of – or as, in an observational situation, s/he's watching what's getting done.

Chapter Four

Discourse

In chapter 3, we were describing the work of writing an institutional ethnography as a sequence of dialogues. There is, first, the interchange between the ethnographer and the experiences of those s/he learns from, the experiencing of the observer, or the researcher's own personal experiences as s/he writes them. Then there is the dialogue drawing on the first and aiming at those who might be the readers of what is to be assembled from what has been learned. The discourse of institutional ethnography is a complex of what those involved in the field write, read, talk about, present at conferences, and so on, as well, of course, as the concepts and terms we have become accustomed to using. In our early work in this general area, we used the concept of "ideology" to bring into view institutional systems of concepts (for example, Smith, 1974; Griffith, 1984; de Montigny, 1995a). But "discourse" became a useful alternative through the work of Michel Foucault (1970, 1972, 1981), which made visible organized practices of using language that formulate and recognize objects of knowledge in ways that are distinctive and differentiating. Discourse, as Foucault uses the term, is applied to standardized, generalized, and generalizing forms of making statements. Statements are the empirical ground of his investigations of discourse. Discourses are *systematically produced*; they are ordered and controlled; those who participate in them have learned from others how to do so. Some cultural theorists include in the notion of discourse any lexically and syntactically specialized language, such as shop-floor talk and pickpockets' jargon as well as political and scientific discourses. Institutional ethnography prefers to stay with Foucault's original conception of discourse as systematically produced, ordered, and disseminated. But while Foucault writes of the order of discourse (1981) and has explored discourse in institutional settings, IE uses the concept of discourse as a tool to recognize those social relations in which the work of many is coordinated by texts. There must always be people who are reading or writing or talking and whose work orients through texts to futures, pasts, and elsewheres and to others never to be encountered except through their written words.

In building on Foucault's conception of discourse, institutional ethnography has extended it into a conceptual space in which institutional ethnographers can recognize a specialization of language uses as going on among people. For institutional ethnography, discourse refers to translocal relations coordinating the practices of definite individuals talking, writing, reading, watching, and so forth, in particular local places at particular times. Participants create texts for other participants to read; they read what others have written and take them into account in their own work. People are active in participating in a discourse, and their participation reproduces and changes it. Though discourse is regulated in various ways, through books such as this for example, each moment of discourse in action both reproduces and changes it. We stress again: discourse is an organization of relations among actual people engaged and active in actual local settings – offices, conferences, workshops, classrooms, homes – whose activities, our work, are coordinated textually.

As a concept useful for opening up what the ethnographer learns and learns from, *discourse* locates a definite mode of the textual coordinating of people's doings, including feelings, that people are active in and that links them to relations overriding their particularities. In the world organized textually, discourses establish among us a known-in-common social context constituted by particular concepts, categories, and methods of building textual representations of actualities. Discourse, then, is not a theory; it does not explain, but directs our ethnographic attention to people – ourselves, for example – who are researching, talking, writing, reading, and learning from each other and coordinating our work. It also directs our attention to concepts originating in discourse that come into play in how institutional practices are organized. In her dissertation, Alison was discovering the "institutional discourse" of the "single-parent family." Both Alison and Dorothy were "single parents" and experienced being defined as defective parents. "The themes of single parent family difference are textually mediated through academic journals, newspapers and magazines, and policy documents" (Griffith, 2006, p. 137). Alison's dissertation (1984) was important to us in developing our understanding of how discourses enter into institutional practices. It shifted our thinking from a basis in what appears in the formal texts of a discourse to opening up how – in governing settings – a discursive language is integral to how institutional practices are organized. We will take another look at that as we describe Gerald de Montigny's work in chapter 8.

As stressed earlier, we have built this book on the basis of what we have learned from the researches of institutional ethnographers (such as ours) – and what we learned in the course of writing and in our inter-changes with each other. We have been active in the IE discourse. Read-ing and writing are textual practices. Our bodies are active in the doing. Step outside this text for a moment. Attend, as you read, to where you are as you are reading. You are where your body is. Whatever time sequences the text may be creating as you activate it in reading, there is the inexora-ble ongoing of what's happening in you and around you, in what you're doing and what's on its way. Your reading is just here; it is what you are, what your body is doing, situated in time, space, and place. And, of course, as Alison or Dorothy write, read, or edit this text, each too is just where she is – sitting as these words appear on her computer monitor, writing at different times, and sending off on the internet her latest addi-tion or editing for her colleague to take a look at. Attending to your bod-ily presence in the act of reading means seeing that reading is a physical act involving the movement of your eyes, of your hands on your mouse or holding the book, of changing pages. Your brain and eyes are active in how you recognize words, translating them into whatever meaning means. There are words that you know, sentences you can follow, and the comfort or discomfort of where you're sitting and the light or lighting of the screen enabling you to read. All this and more and more.

As you read, you engage in a text–reader conversation. Your way of reading, your biography, your tacit knowledge – all are part of how you engage with the text. The text, itself, is not passive. It was written by someone at some time and some where. The text you read or listen to is the product of several work processes (writing, editing, publishing, distribution, and so on). At one point in that production, the author(s) actively selected words, phrases, sentences, decided on the ordering of the argument, wrote in the citations indicating texts the authors have previously read and included in their study. They have done this within a particular genre (e.g., academic, technical, and so on) in order to con-vey something to the reader. As the reader engages with or activates the text, s/he engages with the discourses the text brings forward. In the process, the reader's consciousness is changed. While we all read or lis-ten to texts in our individual everyday lives, we can still say, "Have you read Smith and Griffith's book on institutional ethnography?" In other words, our reading and the texts we read are grounded in the possibili-ties of individual readings of the same text – newspapers, Facebook and Twitter, television shows, audio books, mystery novels, and so on – yet the text itself does not change. It is the same book or article or podcast or movie. We'll come back to the peculiarities of texts in chapter 6.

Discourses are embedded in texts. But they do not disappear when you've stepped out of the text to locate your consciousness in your body. At the moment of reading, you are active in a discourse – one that is shared with others. These words on this page were written as a chapter to a book about institutional ethnography. There are other IE books, quite a few; many papers have been published or presented at conferences; courses have been given at universities. There are people all over the world who are also active in this discourse, though we may not know who, when, or where. We read, we talk, we research and write and think and argue and, as we do, we are engaging with and participating in something like a shared textual community. This textual community is coordinated in distinctive practices of language use that we are learning to or know how to speak or write. In writing or in reading, we are always active in social relations. That is, we enter into sequences of action in which what we are doing in one place and at a particular time coordinates with what others are or will be doing as participants in this discourse elsewhere and elsewhen. In dropping into our bodies as we read or write we are not dumping discourse, not escaping out of a discourse into some simplicity of consciousness that has no words. The discourse is right there in what we're doing.

Recognizing ourselves as being in our bodies locates us where a discourse happens, *as it must*, in what actual people are doing, have done, will do. It locates us in the materiality of the medium coordinating our activities – the texts we read and write, the words, phrases, syntactic arrangements, and so on that we have learned to use and recognize as others use (or do not use – "this is not an institutional ethnography," you might say as you listen to someone presenting an academic paper at a conference). Your action of putting aside a text you had been reading seems to be at odds with still being discursively involved. But as Alison and Dorothy write and edit and as you read, or set aside our text to think, we are all engaged in that strange dialogue, our text–reader conversation, framed by and framing the discourse of institutional ethnography.

The term *discourse* as used here does not apply only to those grounded academically. A rather different use of the concept of discourse can be found in Paul Luken and Suzanne Vaughan's exploration of the public discourse developed in the early twentieth century promoting the single-family, detached, suburban house as the ideal place for bringing up children. Their study deploys the concept of discourse to explore an institutional regime coordinating the activities of people whose various local situations are "drawn into a common set of organizational processes" (Luken and Vaughan, 2014, p. 260). The research began in the

1990s with interviews of women over sixty living in Phoenix, Arizona, focusing on their experience of housing. Luken and Vaughan went on to explore a discourse originating in the work of child welfare experts who were emphasizing the significance of specific local and home physical conditions and furnishing for the best child-rearing – the "Standard American Home (SAH)." Luken and Vaughan's study focuses on the role in establishing the SAH of three state-affiliated agencies, the Children's Bureau, the Own Your Own Home campaign, and the Better Homes in America movement. These agencies did research, published articles in newspapers, produced pamphlets, and so on, linking parents to the views of the child welfare experts, creating and promoting standards of housing related to child-rearing, and connecting them to the projects of suburban housing development being widely undertaken in the United States at that time.

Luken and Vaughan's study includes visual texts reproducing, for example, brochures produced by or for the Children's Bureau, and photographs of houses conforming to the suburban model. They also describe an extension of the SAH discourse into a campaign aimed at promoting home ownership, supported by the US Department of Labor, lumber companies, lending agencies, realtors, and municipalities. In their study we can see the potential power of the concept of discourse to draw together dimensions of the ruling relations that have much to tell us about how they enter into the organizing of people's everyday lives.

Discourse can also be opened up as people's experience. Alison and Dorothy discovered what we came to call the "mothering discourse" as a lurking presence in our lives, which we had not been aware of until we were developing an ethnography of how women's work as mothers complemented the work of teachers in elementary schools (Griffith and Smith, 2005). In our interviews, we focused particularly on the school day. As single parents, both of us had experienced being stereotyped as "defective mothers" at our children's schools (Griffith, 2006). As an accidental by-product of our research, we discovered the presence of this stereotype in our own lives and in our participation in the "mothering discourse." Though we could not identify specific texts or people from whom we had learned how to think and feel about our *work* as mothers, as participants we knew how to define and evaluate our work as well as how to locate ourselves being "single parents" as "defective mothers" in its terms. When our research was well under way, Alison happened to interview a woman who told her how she was involving her children (still in elementary school) in making decisions about which of Shakespeare's plays they should go to at the Stratford Festival in Ontario. She made Alison feel like an "inadequate mother." Alison's experience of being guilty by omission was overwhelming. As a single parent with two children and a very limited income, she could afford neither the time nor the money to take them to Stratford, let alone sit around with them mulling over various Shakespeare plays that they had never had a chance to see. "But why should she feel guilty?" we asked ourselves as we talked this through. Alison was doing a good job – an exceptional job under the circumstances. So we, in a sense, "looked around" to try to find out how we were seen as, and indeed saw ourselves as, defective parents. It was only around that time that feminist historical research had been done that told the history of what we decided to call "the mothering discourse," as it had been developed in the Canadian situation (Arnup, 1994). This new research made us aware of what we had not recognized before, that how we viewed our own responsibilities as mothers, how we responded to the guilting implicit in the institutional identification of "the single parent" (Griffith, 2006), and indeed how we had conceptualized our research project, were all deeply embedded in the framework of the mothering discourse.

We did not become aware of the presence, or even the existence, of what we came to call the mothering discourse until the interviewing stage of our research was already done. Once we could recognize how we participated in that discourse, we could see that we had taken it for granted and built it into how we organized our interviews. In a sense, we had assumed that the mothers we spoke to were also participants in the mothering discourse and would know how to respond in its terms. The mothering discourse connects to a public-school system in which school attendance is legally regulated and in which schools keep track, particularly at the elementary level, of a child's arrival at school. We used the frame of the "school day," starting with the work involved in getting children to school on time and tracking the women's ongoing daily activities as it related to the school and school scheduling. Once Alison's experience had begun to wake us up and we had located the Canadian research on mothering discourse, we could begin to see that we had created a problem and to recognize where we had failed in a couple of interviews in which the woman we talked to didn't respond as a participant in that discourse and didn't recognize *our* participation in it in how she responded.

In order to learn about some of the different ways mothers of children in elementary school were doing the work of mothering, we interviewed mothers at two different income levels, as identified by the school board administration. One interview failure was with a woman Dorothy interviewed who was in our lower income group. The implicit dialogue organization that had built in the assumptions of the mothering discourse somehow just didn't work. It seemed that the woman we interviewed simply did not participate in it. When Dorothy visited her home, she did not seem to care in the least that on both occasions her seven-year-old daughter was home from school, apparently for no reason (the child was not sick); she gave Dorothy no explanation, as a mother participating in the mothering discourse would have done. On her first visit, Dorothy felt that somehow she was asking the wrong questions and using the wrong interview focus. Answers turned into dead-ends. She was getting nowhere. So, she went back for a second time. While she was there, the phone rang, and the woman called out to her daughter: "Don't answer it! Don't answer it! It might be the school." If she had been a participant in the mothering discourse, she would have been too embarrassed to respond as she did in the interviewer's presence. We who are participants in the discourse know that we can be judged by other participants, and clearly the woman Dorothy talked to did not have any problem with her daughter being home from school with no rationale (for further discussion on this example, see Griffith and Smith, 2005).

When we discovered the presence of the mothering discourse in various studies done in the United States and, in particular, Arnup's study of its development in Canada (1994 – Arnup did not use the notion of discourse), we came to see how we had participated in it without being aware we were and that the woman Dorothy interviewed badly was not a participant. If we had seen at the time what we now see so clearly, we would have had to work out how to learn from her about her work life and how she handled her daughter's relation to schooling. We are not sure, even today, how we could have been effective. In our research, we had been committed to the framework of the mothering discourse. Here indeed did the forces of our own lives enter into relations that overpowered us (Marx and Engels, 1973, p. 14).

So here is *discourse* in brief:

- Discourse refers to a specialized practice in reproducible texts that constitutes for participants a world in common.
- It is actively created and distributed textually to engage with those who become participants.
- It constitutes aspects of people's worlds as known, establishing a conceptual order that identifies and connects what become objects of knowledge, and
- It organizes for participants what is to be said, written, or otherwise represented; and in doing so it also excludes.

Chapter Five

Work

We have emphasized that institutional ethnographies are grounded in people's actual lives, their doings, and the conditions and means thereof, and how they coordinate with others. In learning from the experiences of those on whose everyday knowledge an institutional ethnography is built, we are learning about what they do and how they do it. In recognizing the essentially dialogic character of experience, we are always exploring from the standpoint of those we talk to or observe. Our interest enters into and organizes what they bring into focus, but always develops from their standpoint. In learning from their experiences, we look for clues as to how they are entered into the relations beyond those known directly, for example, of schooling and the educational system. Experiential accounts of their "work" in the sense developed below are important in establishing what we can build on in the stage of research when we explore how those relations are put together.

What concepts have institutional ethnographers developed in the course of research that we can build on? One of the most useful orienting concepts that institutional ethnographers have come to deploy in our explorations is the concept of "work." The ordinary understanding of the term is not ours.

> In modern, industrialized society perhaps the most common understanding of the essential characteristic of work is that it is something for which we get paid. This idea is associated with activity in the public world, which is dominated by men and separated from those private worlds of family and personal relationships where women predominate. (Daniels, 1987, p. 403)

Our distinctive usage originated in the Marxist-feminist group, Wages for Housework, that insisted that housework must be recognized as work, that it takes time, effort, and thought, and is done under definite physical and relational conditions (Dalla Costa and James, 1972). Wages for Housework expanded the concept of work to recognize a whole range of unpaid activities, not by any means done exclusively by women. The concept of work understood in this way has been taken up by institutional ethnographers to organize our dialogue with what we learn from talking to people, what we experience ourselves, and what we may observe and learn from others. As we stressed earlier in our critique of established sociologies, typically in most such sociologies, concepts stand in for people's actual activities. However, for institutional ethnography, our chosen concepts are like doors opening up to what actual people are doing in coordination with others. Work is one of the practically useful notions in IE, redesigned as what we call the "generous conception of work." Our generous conception of work serves to make ethnographically observable what people do intentionally (this does not mean they want to do it) that takes effort and time and is done under definite conditions. It makes us aware of discoveries to be made when we are in dialogue with respondents in interviews or other situations of learning for developing an ethnography.

Institutional ethnography's expanded and generous usage of the term "work" opens up aspects of what people do that often will otherwise be missed and go unrecognized in the everyday usage of the word. It is useful for what can be learned from respondents in interviews or from observing. The origins of the conception – indeed, discovering how useful it can be in developing ethnographic data – came from studies done in the very early stages of institutional ethnography's emergence from standard sociologies. In her book *Feeding the Family*, Marjorie DeVault (1991) was critical of the use of the term "work" applied as a model of paid employment. Her study was based on interviews with a number of parents, mostly women, in which she learned how they went about feeding their families. Her discussion in *Feeding the Family* is brilliant in bringing the everyday and ongoing thinking, decision making, shopping, buying, making, and serving food to a family into view. Some of that work is obvious – someone has to shop, someone has to cook, people have to eat. Some is not so obvious – one child doesn't like cheese, another child will only eat toast, her partner doesn't really like vegetables, and nobody but her likes peas. When will the shopping be done? Is there enough milk to last until the next shopping trip or does she have to stop at the store on the way home? "When can I arrange to stop at the supermarket and pick up what I need?" And so on. This whole subjective dimension – thinking, feeling, planning – is incorporated into the generous notion of work as it has built on DeVault's study. Food is also something people do that gets done at particular moments and takes time.

Another important ethnography that set in place a generous conception of work was Tim Diamond's (1992) account drawing on his own
experience of the work of nursing assistants in residences for seniors.
Though the major ethnographic emphasis is on the actualities of what
nurses' aides do and their control by managerial texts, Diamond emphasizes that the seniors were also working. In one instance, he describes
residents of the facility sitting in their wheelchairs, close to the elevator, waiting for breakfast to arrive: "[T]here each sat before breakfast,
bib in place, eyes glued to the elevator. They waited quietly, with a
wild patience, practicing patienthood, actively practicing the skills of
silence" (Diamond, 1992, p. 129). We might remember this when we
have to go to a hospital emergency room and wait, sometimes for several hours, to see a doctor. That is work, and we get pretty skilled at it if
we suffer from a health problem that takes us there often, or simply as
we get older. In such instances, we can look at the work of waiting from
the inside of our own experience. The shift that institutional ethnography has made is how the "generous" conception of work can bring into
view their doings as people know them experientially.

Applying a "generous" concept of work in developing ethnographic
data gets us closer, as DeVault and Diamond have shown, to being able
to bring into view how people are getting things done in the actual situations of their lives. As respondents are entered into the dialogic of their
experience, they can trace back further in memory to discover for the
ethnographer what goes beyond what s/he had expected in preparing
the research. The concept promotes a dialogue that brings out aspects of
what people do in real situations that coordinate with others' work and
hence potentially opens up relations beyond the individual to which their
work is articulated. Making work visible that is not ordinarily recognized
as such opens up directions for discovering what people know they do
and know how to do, and hence their work implicitly or explicitly carries
connections with sequences of action beyond the individual. In exploring
federally funded job training for immigrant women in the United States,
Kamini Maraj Grahame (1998) was dealing with complex institutions. In
developing her inquiry, she interviewed those working in a variety of
institutional sites. She opened her interviews with a question focusing on
the respondent's work: "What do you do?" What they told her of the actual work they were doing was, of course, different in different sites and
for those with differing responsibilities, but by getting them to open up
about the work they were doing, she also brought into view the texts that
generalized across many settings of the administration of job training.

At many moments in what we have written earlier in this book, we
have referred to research we had done exploring the work mothers

do in relation to their children's schooling (Griffith and Smith, 2005). We used the notion of work as a way to bring into view the everyday activities of mothers with children in elementary school. When we began our research on mothering for schooling, we thought we had a pretty good handle on women's mothering work. We were both mothers. We had children in school. Of course, as mothers, we had talked with other mothers about our children and ourselves. We started our research project by interviewing each other to discover areas we didn't know enough about. Then we started interviewing our respondents and began indeed to discover how little we knew. Some of our ignorance was a simple and typical problem that is encountered when doing ethnography – some things were so familiar we just forgot to pay attention to them; for example, getting children up in the morning and getting them off to school. Of course we knew how to do that and what was required. As we asked mothers to tell us about their morning routines, we began to wonder how it was possible that they were all so similar – getting up, dressed, breakfast (or not), teeth cleaned, shoes on and tied, jackets on, lunches in hand, and out the door in time to walk to school and get there before the bell rings. The detail of the mothering work routines as we learned about them from those we interviewed was distinctive to each family; yet despite the differences in the morning routines from family to family, the standard end point was getting the children to school "before the bell rings."

An example from our data: Ms Arthur is a nurse who does shifts at the local hospital. Her husband is a millwright, whose job begins at 6 a.m., meaning he has to leave home at 5:30 in order to get to work on time. Daycare centres do not open until at least 7 a.m. School starts at 8:45. When Ms Arthur is on the graveyard shift and working until 7:30 a.m., she hires a babysitter to come in at 5 a.m. and get the children ready and take them to school by 8:45. The babysitter is hired essentially to link the family–school relation when the parents cannot do the work of getting the children to school on time. Note here, in this example, we have the family's relation to the labour market: Ms Arthur and her husband must also pay attention to the requirements of their jobs – graveyard shifts, early morning starts. Neither their jobs nor the school pay attention to the lack of fit. These institutional relations are coordinated across families, across jobs. It's the family, typically the mother, whose morning routines must bend to accommodate such disjunctures.

What we had thought of as simply a group of morning routines done by mothers with children began to come into view as a set of coordinated activities shaped by both the labour market – the work day; and the school – the school day. Of course there are other social relations engaged here, but we do not have several hours – or days – to open up every connection for exploration. We will stick with the family–school relation coordinated, in part, by the ordinary morning activities of getting children off to school on time. What is the next link in this family–school relation – the institutional relation? Here, we need to bring into view another concept, another window into the institutional relation we are exploring, and this is the notion of text to be taken up in the following chapter. Can you see what's going on in the family–school relation? All the action, at least on a "typical school day," was being done in relation to somewhere else. There is an invisible partner to the "getting-off-to-school" work of the mother and her children. Of course, the invisible partner that is shaping their ordinary morning work is the school. Getting to school on time before the bell rings. Most of the family's morning work on weekdays coordinates the timing and much of the action going on each morning with the aim of arriving at school on time. The school is an invisible participant in the weekday morning work of the family.

Once we begin working with a notion of work in the generous sense, much can become visible that we would not have known to look for in our ethnographic dialogue with those we learn from in our research. There is, for example, a whole region of work in this sense that involves a transfer of work from paid wage-workers to unpaid workers who are not recognized as doing work. Nona Glazer's book (1993) on women's paid and unpaid labour unveils the history of the supermarket. In the days when customers did not walk up and down the aisles picking out what they wanted to buy, everything was done by the sales clerk, owner, or paid employee, who searched the shelves of the "store" for what customers asked for and brought it to them on the counter or arranged to have it delivered. Around 1912, a grocery store in the United States invented the self-service store now so familiar to us. In any store we go into now, the work of finding the stuff on the shelves and toting it down to the checkout is the customers' work. It's no longer the work of the sales people and other staff to go and find things for you. You take it home, walking, busing, or driving, and that is work too (Glazer, 1993, pp. 48–67). Though at any particular time in the research, the ethnographer may be focusing on what a particular individual is doing and experiencing, there are always, as can be seen in our account of our "mothering for schooling" research, implicit relations connecting that work to others' doings/work. That connectedness is an important dimension of what institutional ethnographers explore. In many of our actions, those connections are invisible to us or we pay them no attention. Yet, we are very much connected. When going to the supermarket, for example, to pick up what you need to make dinner at home, you have entered an extraordinarily complex organization of social relations. It is likely that you don't know or don't pay attention to the complexity of what is going on behind your back. Our supermarket experience takes place not only with the clerks in the store, not only with the people who are doing the shelving, but also with a range of complex social relations. Goodness knows where those products on the shelves were produced or how they got there. Goodness knows what the processes of production were. All that complex organization is something that is mediated by this moment of interpersonal exchange of money and the collection of dinner ingredients (becoming commodities in the monetary abstraction) dumped on the moving surface that edges them towards the cash register. We do not usually see last-minute dinner shopping as connecting us with others beyond those present in the store with us who are also shopping, and the cashiers. But it does.

We have come to take using an automated teller machine (ATM) for granted. Glazer gives us some background history. Historically, bank tellers filled out withdrawal and deposit slips for bank customers, but in the 1950s the banks began putting deposit and withdrawal slips out on counters. A teller's work then shifted from filling in the forms to checking the customer's work and teaching customers how to fill in the forms accurately. Thus, the customer's work was expanded to include form filling (Glazer, 1993, p. 19). And as the customer's work of interchange with her or his bank becomes electronic, either via the ATM or the debit card machine at the store or managing a bank account on the internet, we as customers are indirectly implicated in the displacement of paid employees. This shifting of work from paid to unpaid is one of the aspects of social relations that do not appear as relations between people, yet are so; they operate in people's lives in powerful ways. This was brought home to Dorothy when she was waiting in line at the bank one day and overheard a couple of tellers chatting with each other about how they had moved from bank to bank as banks closed, relating the closures to the use of automatic tellers and "electronic banking." With technologies advancing in multiple areas, our unpaid work is increasingly displacing paid work. In supermarkets today, cash registers and the clerk at the desk are being displaced with machines – pretty inept as yet, but getting there. As this happens, people's relations to others change imperceptibly. Our social world is reorganized. We can find examples of these kinds of things all around us if we start looking for them.

Institutional ethnography's generous conception of *work* has, however, an even deeper reach into what people do that, as emphasized above, takes time, effort, and is intended as, but cannot so easily be seen as, work. Mykhalovskiy (2002) and McCoy (2002) in their collaborative researches used the concept of "healthwork" in their explorations of the work of people living with HIV. Here is how the concept of "healthwork" oriented their research:

> The term healthwork helped guide our interviews in the sense of directing our attention to the range of activities that PHAs [people having AIDS] engage in around HAART [highly active anti-retroviral therapy] without presupposing, in advance, a set of relevant activities such as "informed decision making" or reinscribing normative conceptions of what those activities should be. (Mykhalovskiy, 2008, p. 141)

It is clear that their ethnographic project is one of discovery; they did not know before their research just what "healthwork" would look like. They came to envisage their ethnographies as creating

> a kind of map or overview of the range of activity that PHAs [people having AIDS] engage in as part of looking after their health. We want to make visible the often invisible work that PHAs do around their health. ... [aiming at] creating a picture of the range activities that PHAs engage in as part of looking after themselves. (McCoy and Mykhalovskiy, 2002, p. xii)

Notice how their project as a process of discovery came to aim at being open to "the range of practices and activities" of people. What these might be were not specified or categorized in advance. They made sure, however, that those with whom they talked in interviews and focus groups came from a variety of social backgrounds. They did not use these variations as a sample characterizing the properties of a population, but simply to learn about some of the different ways PHAs were doing their healthwork. They were thus able to develop some sense of the *range* of respondents' practices.

In standard qualitative methods in sociology, the direction of research is already theoretically prescribed. Mykhalovskiy and McCoy worked with a very different strategy. Though they began with some definite topics to explore, they discovered the directions their research was taking in the process of doing it. In a later paper, Mykhalovskiy describes how their research took shape as they learned from those they talked with:

> Over time, our interviews came to focus on four main zones of practice or work. These included medication practices (e.g., taking pills, developing and modifying medication routines), dealing with health care practitioners (e.g., finding doctors, developing relationships with them, educating

them), learning about HIV and its treatment (observing and listening to other people with HIV, gathering and interpreting textual and other sources of information, etc.), and experiences of coming to take (or not take) combination therapy. ... (Mykhalovskiy, 2008, p. 141)

Though a concept such as "work" or "healthwork" orients the direction of research, we can see from McCoy and Mykhalovskiy's study how what it came to refer to was worked out in the research process as they were learning from those they talked with. At the same time, the concept does organize what is brought into view: it is what is actually being done by people; it focuses on how they care for their bodies; it points to links with health care institutions; and so on. As Mykhalovksiy stresses, concepts applicable to the same general situation such as "informed decision-making" just would not bring into view what they were able to learn from their respondents. Indeed, the title of the group-authored collection to which McCoy and Mykhalovskiy contributed their research is "making care visible" (Bresalier et al., 2002).

The ordinary invisibility of work in the extended or generous sense means that when we are doing interviews, we have to find ways of getting people to talk about the work they do in the IE sense, without being stuck with the everyday meaning of the term or its meaning in economics and political economy, that is, as something done for pay. Indeed, it is best to avoid using the word "work" with respondents, because they will naturally understand it as it is ordinarily used, not as it is used in IE. A typical problem of getting people to talk about their work in the IE sense arises in interviewing professionals, managers, and administrators: they could be teachers, they could be occupational therapists; they could be doctors; they could be store managers. In telling you, the ethnographer, about what they do in their work, they use the words of their profession, its institutional discourse; characteristically, their language does not refer to the specifics of what they actually do.

> In interviews, it is common – and understandable – that people in an institutional setting describe their work using the language of the institution. This is especially the case with people who have been taught a professional discourse as part of their training or people whose work requires them to provide regular accounts of institutional processes. ... The challenge for the institutional ethnographer is to recognize when the informant is using institutional language. (DeVault and McCoy, 2006, p. 37)

For example (to be further described in chapter 7), Alison noticed how teachers in Ontario often refer to their students as "level 2s" or "level 3s."

The reference here is to the students' rank within the four achievement levels of the standardized test. When a teacher refers to her students in this discursive manner (as, say, Level 2s), she is identifying students who require extra help in the classroom to raise their test scores. But her extra work with the Level 2s disappears into the category, which simply references the student achievement level. Contrast this with Dorothy's experience a while ago when she was doing a study with steelworkers. She was interested in how they learned the skills involved in their jobs. One of the extraordinary things she found out was that she experienced no difficulty with them telling her about what might be called the "work" of learning skills or of teaching other workers. They spoke very freely and concretely about how they learned, and some spoke also of how they passed on their knowledge to others. They spoke at length about that work and were very detailed. There was no institutional genre of language displacing the concrete details of what they were getting done. When respondents whose jobs are institutionally defined speak in their institutional genre, encourage them to give examples from their experience, to just describe what is or has to be done, and so on. That will help to bring discursive abstractions down to earth (more about that language in chapter 7). Your dialogue with respondents brings the most value to your ethnography because it makes what they do/their work – in the generous sense – observable to themselves as well as to you – as their actual doings.

Chapter Six

Texts

Institutional ethnographies are built on what the ethnographer learns about what actual people do or are doing. But they would not work if what was recorded assimilated people's doings to themselves as individuals. Concepts of standard sociologies such as "role" do just this. But institutional ethnography always looks beyond an individual's activity to learn how what they do coordinates with what others have been or will be doing. Coordinating our doings with others does not mean only what people do when others are present. When someone having breakfast alone pulls up a chair and sits down with knife and fork and plate before him- or herself, with legs under the table, this solitary action is still oriented towards others' presences and doings in how it is getting done and in what is being eaten. Pierre Bourdieu (1950) introduced the concept of *habitus* to displace notions such as "social structure," in which the presence of people as agents disappears. It gives us a way of thinking about how the ordinary concerting of people's doings with those of others becomes built into our bodily dispositions as these are learned in our everyday life experiences. At the same time, it creates the problem of reducing the ongoing coordinating of people's doings into properties of individuals. Beyond Bourdieu, or evading him, institutional ethnography, as we have emphasized earlier, wants more than people's readiness to do; it wants them in action, wants to learn what they are doing, and how that *coordinates with what others have been doing or will be doing*. When we are learning from our respondents in the field, we orient our interest not just to what they do, but we also have in mind discovering sequences of action beyond the individual. What a particular individual has to tell us about her or his work opens up connections to social relations beyond their direct experiential knowledge. Thus, we do not adopt concepts like "role" to attach what people do to them as individuals, and we are comfortable with Bourdieu's notion of *habitus* while setting aside how it also ties us down to individuals rather than people's actions in relation to others. We want to move as Marx and Engels (1973, 1976) did, that is, towards discovering how people's actual doings articulate to relations that overpower their lives. We want to learn what actual people are doing, but always as it coordinates with others' doings.

To enter ethnographically into the ruling relations, we have come to recognize and attend to how texts as material objects (electronic as well as print) carrying messages of various kinds coordinate what people do across multiple sites and times. Texts, then, are not seen as an independent focus of investigation, as they are, for example, in discourse analysis in its multiple forms. They are always to be recognized for how they coordinate what is being done as a moment in a sequence of action among people – a social relation. Texts are not to be divorced from how they actually come into play as a part of people's work – as they are being made or activated. The ethnographer must always have people present. People themselves can describe what they do with a text – with filling in a form, for example, or giving an account of how a text was put together, or how it was being read as a moment in a course of action. Or the ethnographer may be observing how a given text comes into play in a court of law, in a religious ceremony, or is being written in the course of negotiating the making of a policy (Eastwood, 2006, 2018). Texts, for the institutional ethnographer, make visible the distinctive forms of coordinating people's work (in the IE sense) that is constitutive of institutional and large-scale organization – the relations of ruling. By tracing the actual activities of people as their work is coordinated with and through texts, the institutional ethnographer can explore the ruling relations *from within the everyday of people's experience.*

In developing an ethnographic exploration of ruling relations, George Smith provided a useful account of how the notion of the more general term "social relations" should be used. He tells us that:

> [T]he notion of social relations ... is not a thing to be looked for in carrying out research, rather, it is what is used to do the looking.' ... [I]t is employed in a practical manner to talk about and to investigate the actual practices of individuals, articulated to one another, in courses of action where different moments are dependent upon one another and are articulated to one another not functionally but reflexively, as temporal sequences in which the foregoing intends the subsequent and in which the subsequent realizes or accomplishes the social character of the preceding. (G.W. Smith, 1995, p. 24)

Institutional ethnography avoids dissociating texts from actual sequences of action. Texts do not act; they come into play in individuals' work as they coordinate the foregoing and subsequent moments of a sequence of action. Dorothy has described writing her recipe, and when she thinks of cooking that dish again, she goes back to what she had written to read what she had written as instructions. The district attorney in Duluth, Minnesota (where Ellen Pence did much of her remarkable work) reads a report written by the police who responded to a domestic abuse call. Having in mind the Minnesota law, the officer has to figure out if this report meets its specifications and thus requires her to issue charges against someone for an offence. A student will start at Langara College in the fall, but in the early summer she struggles on her iPad to get signed up for the courses she wants to take. When someone dies, it's not enough to tell the bank where s/he had her or his account; whoever is contacted tells the messenger that the bank needs to see the official death certificate. Dorothy gets on a bus in Vancouver and pats her Compass card against the electronic register. Representatives of different nations involved in UN environmental negotiations struggle with and argue about just what terms should appear in the final document representing their agreement. The chair of a university department is working on a job description for a new professor for the department; s/he needs to know if the graduate students who are represented in the decision-making processes of the department are required to participate in formulating the job description; the fat books of the constitution are sitting on the bottom shelf – better check them to make sure s/he gets it right. And so on and so on. Keep in mind then that texts are to be taken up only as they are used in coordinating what people are actually or will be doing.

Recognizing the activated presence of texts as they are entered into sequences of action is an important ethnographic step. Notice how they are to be conceived only as they become articulated with something people are doing – reading, writing, watching, or listening to or even just referring to a text. In many discourses dealing with texts, they are taken as independent of the actual practices bringing them into play in particular places at some particular time of reading, writing, and so on. Looking for, noting, or otherwise becoming aware of a text as activated in someone's work orients the ethnographer to how that work is coordinated textually with the previous and subsequent work of others. Figure 1 is a visualization of the work–text–work that is in many ways foundational to institutional ethnography's capacity to reach into ruling relations ethnographically.

Ironically, Dorothy had an experience of being challenged to work with texts separated from sequences of action. Ellen Pence asked her to

Figure 1. Text as coordinating a sequence of action

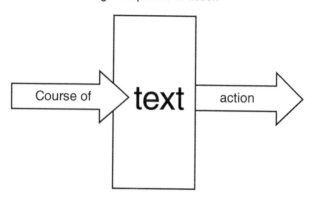

analyse two psychological reports designed to evaluate the psychological status of two women for family court decisions in custody cases.
Dorothy took the IE injunction to avoid detaching texts from people's
action seriously, but she had no way of connecting either report with
the women involved or the psychologist or psychologists who prepared the reports, or to learn what had subsequently happened in the
family court, if and when the reports had been taken into account. She
found, however, and used in her analysis of the psychological reports,
that they could be taken up as texts implicated in a sequence in which
the women whose clinical status was described met with the psychologists, and talked with them in face-to-face sessions. In the texts of the
two reports were traces of, clues to, some of what had been going on
in the sessions between the psychologists and the women on which
the reports were grounded. The women's responses in those sessions
to their situations in the custody case and to the psychologist were the
resources for the psychologists writing the psychological report des-
tined for the custody case hearing. Dorothy's analysis tracks from the
text of the reports to what can be discerned about how the sessions
were organized, and how whatever went on there is translated in the
reports into a one-sided account of the women's behaviour framed in
the language of a clinical psychological discourse. Going after the next
moment in the sequences in which the texts would be read, her analysis
then explores the texts for how the clinically framed reports structure
potential text–reader conversations in which the reader is not assumed
to be a practitioner of the clinical discourse. The reports were texts that
were produced in and articulated to sequences of action in the family
court proceedings in which the child custody decisions would be made.

Figure 2. Work–text–work sequence of action

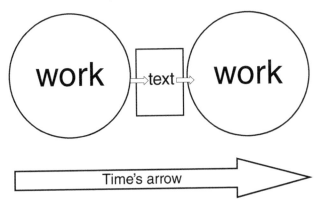

And Dorothy's analysis of how they were written located them in just that institutional sequence.

The diagrammatic forms we use in Figure 2 above to elucidate the work–text–work sequence are those introduced by Susan Turner in her innovative mapping method. We will discuss her work a little further on; for now, here is a diagram of the work–text–work sequence (Figure 2) – always keeping in mind that when we talk about work, we mean the "generous" conception of work elaborated in the previous chapter.

Locating the institutionally coordinating texts and how they are entered into sequences of action is a particularly effective way of exploring ruling relations as they are coordinated and concerted by texts/documents. Institutional texts are constructed to generalize across many local sequences. When they are activated, texts can be taken up as they enter into and become a presence in coordinating actual temporal sequences of action. Thus, when we are learning about someone's work experience that incorporates references to a text or texts as an integral aspect of the work (in the generous sense of course), we are also discovering a potential research direction. The text that can be seen as activated at one moment in a social relation hooks up at the next in a sequence as it is activated in someone else's work in a "work–text–work sequence." The following is an account of work in which a text is directly involved. Shauna Janz (2009) describes the new textually coordinated work of two of her co-workers, Elle and Nadine (not their real names), as well as her own changed work experience following the introduction of new accreditation procedures into a social service agency contracted by the government in British Columbia:

> Elle and Nadine ... reorganize their work and interactions with clients to meet the measurable requirements for writing a good report. In their talk about their work and reporting, a palpable tension surfaces in their descriptions of reading the report back to the client. Every report that is written requires the signature of the client – providing the evidence of 'client-centered planning' that accreditation demands. Both workers talk about the fear of hurting the client's feelings when reviewing behavioral measures that they have tracked for the report that they have to write and subsequently share. This tension plays out in the work of reporting as workers struggle to reconcile meeting the quantitative and measurable expectations for good report writing while keeping in mind that their client will also be reading this report. To gain a trusting relationship with them, I would often re-interpret and paraphrase the report in more friendly language, rather than let the client read it or have me read it verbatim. For example, rather than tell Ted that he had declined in his appropriate behaviors by 70% from the last reporting period because he rated mostly 'fours' and 'fives' on his tracking chart, I would reflect back to specific interactions we had and review which behaviors needed more work and learning in his social interactions. Regardless, I left from these interactions with clients feeling disheartened, confused and internally conflicted in my work and relations with the people I supported. (Janz, 2009, pp. 81–2)

Janz's account of the sequence coordinated by the "tracking charts" of individual clients that agency workers were required to produce opens and directs a line of inquiry it does not tell us where exactly to look to learn more. But it does introduce an account of the agency employees' work, which carries an implicit reference to a subsequent moment. The text (the report) produced is activated in their work as they fit the actualities to the constraints of the text. Janz's ethnography shows us that as we incorporate texts into our institutional ethnographies, it is the texts that hook us up and hook those whose work experience we learn from into the textually ordered relations that generalize across local settings and times and particular people. This is what is referred to in the adjective "institutional" in the name of our discourse.

Here, however, is only a beginning. Our research resources may not allow us to track the work organization of the sequence all the way, because this would involve a trail of interviews that might not be achievable. But we would be able to learn something of the managerial order imposed on the agency making reports of client progress and how that has reorganized the agency's contractual relation to the provincial government, and hence its funding. The research work itself, beginning with an account of actions that involve a particular institutional text, gives IE research a direction that is not fully specified in advance. It is to be discovered as the research proceeds.

Janz's account of the work of producing accounts of clients' progress directs exploration into what we might call a managerial hierarchy. Her work incorporated the evaluating of a client's progress in a report to be taken up and read by those responsible for assembling such texts into the relevant managerial frame. But, of course, not all accounts of people's work involving texts orients in that direction.

A different direction is taken by Ellen Pence (2001), whose major focus was the judicial processing of cases of domestic abuse in Minnesota – what George Smith (1988) called a "mandated course of action." "Mandated" refers to the institutional authorization by law and other modes of regulation of a sequence of action coordinating across organizational units, such as police, city attorney, courts, and jails and other legal penalties (Minnesota had introduced a law that criminalized "domestic abuse"). Authorized texts are foundational in that they are written in a standardized and standardizing language that can be applied to various particularities of local events and doings.

The "domestic abuse" sequence begins with the emergency call and the police response. A key moment in the sequence is how police on patrol handled calls that might be identifiable legally as a case of "domestic abuse" and how what they learned was represented in the reports that were produced. Pence traces the report at its point of origin as a verbal recording by the officers involved through its transcription and then review and approval by the supervisor, at which point it becomes official. The replicated text then travels through a series of what Pence calls "processing interchanges" in which the work of different agencies in the institutional order comes into play and is coordinated. Below is an account transcribed from a detective's sketch of a sequence of such interchanges, starting with the report of a police squad's response to "a domestic tracing" – what can be recognized as a temporal sequence, much as George Smith recommends. The squad produces a report; the supervisor reviews it; it then goes to the traffic division where someone logs it as a "warrant request." At each interchange, the text of the domestic abuse report arrives and informs a local work process and can be taken up into actions mandated by the relevant institutional position and then passed on to the next processing interchange in the mandated sequence.

Jan. 1, 1993, a Friday: A domestic between a co-habiting couple occurs in the city. The victim gets a black eye and bloody nose and calls the police.

A sqd. responds and finds the offender gone and is not able to locate him within the 4 hours. They go back to their business.

Jan. 2: The sqd. dictates a report.

Jan. 4: The report is transcribed and returned to the Patrol division.

Jan. 7: The report is signed by the supervisor and taken to the traffic division where it is logged as a warrant request.

Jan. 8: It is placed in the city attorney basket. It is Friday.

Jan. 11: It is logged into the city attorney's office and sent to an attorney. Some time within the next couple of weeks, an attorney will review it, decide to issue [a summons], direct a clerical to fill out the necessary forms.

Jan. 25: The file is returned to the DPD Detective Bureau clerical person with a summons attached.

Jan. 27: The clerical types out the summons information and mails the package out, including all of the reports, the victim and witness information and statements.

Jan. 28: The victim and offender, having continued to live together, share the first day since the assault that they have not thought or argued about it.

Jan. 29: The offender opens his mail and notes that his court date is set for Feb. 22. (Pence, 2001, p. 220)

At more than one of these work sites, an account of the actual work done there would likely suggest lines of investigation analogous to how we have taken up Janz's account. For example, the city attorney site would presumably be where the police report would have to be checked with the wording of Minnesota's "domestic abuse" legislation if charges were to be issued. Pence's exploration, however, directs us to recognize sequences in which a particular text may "travel," coordinating the work being done at different sites in the sequence. As it travels, additional texts such as a "warrant" to make an arrest may be added that enter the original textual representation into institutional action. What begins as a report is foundational to what becomes an institutional "case" or "file" as actions taken at sequential interchanges are recorded. The "case" as it is developed represents, in texts written in the relevant institutional language, the institutionally relevant history of the actual person charged with the offence.

A third example draws attention to textually ordered relations knitting people's work across institutional boundaries. Rashmee Karnad-Jani (2015) has explored the work required of South Asian mothers in the Greater Toronto Area (GTA) in relation to their children's schooling. She focuses particularly on the student course selection process required by the Ministry of Education for all students moving into Grade 9 at a secondary school. Here is Karnad-Jani's summary of the ministry text requiring parents to become active in shaping the direction of their children's education through the work of selecting future courses for their Grade 8 child in the province's public school system:

> [Parents] are required to acquaint themselves with course pathways, course codes, and various terminologies of transition as well as learn the difference between possible course combinations. They are also required to fill registration forms correctly for admission to the high school so that their child can get checked off the Grade 8 teacher's class list. If they make errors in filling these forms, they have to locate them on the school boards' website, download and fill them in correctly. They have to find relevant information about the various courses and pathways. They have to make appointments with their child's teachers or the Special Education Resource Teacher if they have specific questions related to course selection. (Karnad-Jani, 2015, p. 9)

As can be seen, the ministry takes no responsibility for informing parents about the "course pathways," et cetera, let alone about the future career significance of choices made about course combinations. Course selection decisions of either the applied or academic pathways organize students' secondary education experience, and eventually, their entry into higher education and the labour market. Parents are required to do the bureaucratic paper (or electronic) work. It is simply assumed that they have the needed know-how. No account is taken of possible differences among parents' skills and knowledge of how school outcomes relate to future job opportunities. The texts available to parents are only available online and include the Regional Course Directory in which the courses and the pathways are described (there has been no print copy since 2014). Parents who are new to the English language, who are unfamiliar with negotiating the internet, or whose educational background is minimal experience special problems. These are the parents Karnad-Jani worked with in developing her ethnography. Parents consulted teachers and other parents as they figured out the form and how to select courses. They worked interdependently to place students on the applied or academic pathways that would organize their future secondary school experience. Both parents and teachers had to find out how to fit the needed work time into already busy schedules. This textually governed relation extends virtually out of the Ministry of Education through the Board of Education to the local school and the everyday work of teachers coordinated with the work of parents managing their children's relation to public education. We can see here how what we might describe as a "governing" text coordinates peoples' work across institutional boundaries.

The anchorage of these ethnographies of textually organized sequences of action has been the disjunctures between the standard and standardizing texts of ruling and the local actualities of the work being done by those whose work they organize. Now we turn to an institutional ethnography that does something a bit different; in moving to Susan Turner's innovations in the mapping of institutional relations, we encounter a significant shift. From her investigations and analysis, she built a "map" of the translocal work processes producing a municipal land-development *decision*. Turner's mapping of the organization of that decision began when she received a notice from her municipality informing her of a proposed housing development for a ravine close to where she lived. "Residents" were invited to participate by being present in person at the council's meeting where the municipal *decisions* would be made. Susan attended – and recorded – the council session. She became aware of the distinctive institutional language that was spoken and that the text on the basis of which a decision would be made had a complex history of text-coordinated sequences of work involving developers, lawyers, banks, real estate agents, residents, government officials, and land surveyors (Turner, 2006, p. 140). We reproduce here Turner's italicizing of the word *decision*. She does so to preserve the reference to how the ordinary wording describing governmental actions conceals what the institutional ethnographer makes observable – the complex sequence of action in which people are at work reading, writing, and speaking with others, transmitting texts for others to review, reviewing texts sent to them, and so on.

> Mapping actual sequences of work and texts extends ethnography from people's experience and accounts of their experience into the work processes of institutions and institutional action. It is a formulation and application of institutional ethnography that treats quite literally its central concepts of text-based social relations and texts as essential coordinators of institutions. It recognizes the extraordinary capacity of texts to produce and to organize people's activities and extended and general relations in local and particular sites. Mapping institutions as work and text is unlike other forms of graphical mapping of organizations and institutions. It does not produce, for example, a chart of organizational structure. ... Rather the analytic procedure results in an account of the day-to-day text-based work and local discourse practices that produce and shape the dynamic ongoing activities of an institution. (Turner, 2006, p. 139)

Turner's mapping procedure is visual, as can be seen in the diagram reproduced in Figure 3. She introduced circles to represent "work" where people are active and rectangles to represent texts. Her mapping of work–text–work sequences explicates as actual people's doings the objectified and objectifying organization of ruling relations as they "produce their actions as accountable in the terms of the particular process and institution" (Turner, 2006, p. 143) (see Figure 3). She herself became active as a "resident" in the ongoing sequence of action she explored and her map locates her point of entry. The very extensive map is reproduced here so you can get an idea of how it looks. The whole map is so detailed and extensive that it is not readable here. When Dorothy first encountered it at a meeting to discuss Turner's dissertation progress, she was confronted with a huge roll of paper – the map of the municipality processing a development application as people's work–text–work organized activities.

Turner wrote this account of how the map was created:

> I originally did the mapping work by hand. I taped together large sheets from newsprint drawing pads and taped them to the wall in my living room. I added texts, activities, syntactical moves, and phrases as I encountered them – as planners, councillors, developers, and others talked about them. They were read or at hand in public settings, or they were referred to in some other text and so on – and as they went on in time. I included texts people talked about, produced, read, and wrote. The map was approximately 12 feet long by 5 feet high. Reducing it to book page size makes it virtually unreadable, but I want you to be able to see the complexities that mapping can explore and represent as [1]well as how much had gone before and occurred after the point at which the residents intervened. (Turner, 2006, p. 146)

We emphasize that the term "mapping" is not used here as a metaphor; Turner's is a cartographic method of representing actual text–work–text sequences. In illustrating institutional action as a map, her method explicates the actual organization of people's work. From her account, we can begin to see how the ethnographer's work of mapping selects and abstracts from the local actualities to disclose the organization of the *institutional* sequence of action. The mapping procedure is itself integral to unveil what is hidden but foundational to governmental action.[1]

---

1 If you are interested in learning to use Turner's mapping method, visit the website www.mappingforchange.ca.

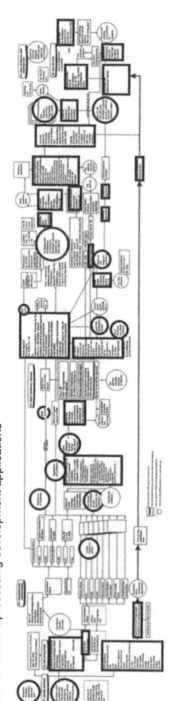

Figure 3. Turner's processing development applications

The extensive mapping method Susan Turner has developed and used so effectively for her research work with her associates on the policing of sexual violence on the Six Nations Reserve (see chapter 10) has other, simpler uses in thinking through a research project. Alison taught graduate courses on IE in York University's Faculty of Education before her retirement. The students in these courses were primarily teachers, with a smattering of educational administrators. Mapping, in this context, was a means to discovering the problematic of their research for the course. Students would begin with a topic they were interested in – something that came out of their everyday work as educators. Drawing from their experiential knowledge, they began to develop maps of "what's going on" in their particular area of interest. For example, suspended and expelled high school students must go through a long bureaucratic process that begins with a particular event that occurs in the classroom or the playground. Whatever occurred only becomes an incident when the educator or school staff report the event to the principal's office. At the principal's discretion (likely supported by a review of the student's school record, which has been built up over the years of schooling), the principal writes a report that is then reviewed through school procedures and subsequently forwarded to the Board of Education. If the incident is deemed to be serious enough, then other bureaucratic and legal procedures come into play that end up in a legal hearing involving the parents and the reporting teacher and principal, as well as the principal from the expelled and suspended school program to which the student is to be assigned.

This is a brief and incomplete description that needs filling out to make clear all of the steps of the process – who is involved at what stage (Note that the parents and the offending student are rarely involved in the meetings except at the beginning and end of the process), and what happens at the end of the process (Is the student expelled or suspended for a given length of time, and which school she/he will attend and for how long?). Here is the beginning of a map of the process the graduate student researcher could then take up, depending on their research plan. When extended, mapping can be used to explicate a complex process, as Susan Turner's work exemplifies. It is also useful in more limited sequences because it pins down how authorized texts coordinate the local process of social relations of ruling. As a research procedure, generally, mapping opens up governmental process to ethnographic research.

PART THREE

The Ethnographic Dialogue

Chapter Seven

Transition to the Ethnography

In this section (Part III) of the book we move from learning from people about their work and how it is coordinated with that of others to bringing into view some of what institutional ethnographers have been discovering as they organize their research and bring together as an ethnography what they have learned and are learning. In this chapter we give particular attention to the language and texts that become "active" in organizing the work of building an ethnography. Chapter 8 engages with the concerns and interests of the ethnographers that have entered into and organized the courses of their exploration. We use the notion of "problematic" to direct attention to how the ethnographers' concerns and interests organized their research direction. In chapter 9, we introduce some of the discoveries that have been made about the distinctive ways the "institutional" texts and the language they carry organize the local actualities of people's doings as they enter institutional courses of action.

   This section of our book draws on and describes some of what has been learned as institutional ethnographers discovered how ruling relations are actually being put together as people are directly active in them. We want to move our discussion from what we've called the "primary" stage, where we are learning directly from people: what they have to tell us, what we can observe, what we can read in the texts that are in play, what we know from our own experience, and so on. Now what we want to bring forward for you is what we see as some of the useful ways researchers have developed research directions that build the ethnography they write for others to read. The two dialogic moments, first of learning from people's experience of what they do and then of writing an ethnography, are not a straightforward sequence the way the general sociological practice of first collecting data and then "analysing" it is. Rather, we may think of the ethnography being built in a process which may involve going back and forth between the developing account of how people's doings are coordinated, the ethnographic dialogue, and the everyday knowledge of individual respondents that is the data source of the ethnography. Indeed, if we look again at Turner's mapping (chapter 6), we can see how a work of learning from respondents about their work and the coordinating texts integrates what, in other research contexts, are different moments in making an ethnography.

We have made no attempt to do a survey of what institutional ethnographers are doing; nor do we claim to open up all the possible and fascinating discoveries that have been and are being made. We have drawn only on our own familiarities with and recollections of our reading to bring forward something of what we have learned about how to go to work as institutional ethnographers and what they have been discovering. Sociology of all kinds enters bravely into exploring and/or explaining a world the complexities of which are expanded by the distinctive ways in which we share and are active in what we seek to know. Standard sociologies handle this problem of societal complexity by using theories to organize, select, and interpret whatever is going on among the people who have become the research focus. The positioning and interests of the researcher are displaced; they may be secretly present in her or his choice of topic, even of theory, but the genre rules of established sociology's secondary dialogue preclude the researcher's interests and point of view from being directly involved in the research design and subsequent writing up.

Institutional ethnography uses concepts to bring into view what we have learned as useful openings into discovering how people are putting things together; how they are coordinating their doings with others. Writing an institutional ethnography starts out in the same world where we ourselves are in our bodies, and hence in a world that is always in process, but it calls for shifts away from the local particularities of what was actually going on with our respondents or those we were observing, to writing an account that draws the different pieces together without describing them in detail. The ethnography writes into a text a representation that is essentially static and re-readable, though it draws on resources grounded in people's actual doings.

Thus the move to writing the ethnography involves taking up the data as it brings into view not just what individuals do, but how what they do coordinates with others' doings (feelings and thoughts are not excluded, but they are understood and learned about because they are involved in and are part of people's doings). Interviewing respondents and exploring with them their experiential knowledge of how they go about getting things done means that our basic data is organized individually. And what we learn is also always from the respondent's standpoint. Though, in a sense, their accounts could be described as "subjective," our dialogue with them will aim at getting concrete and specific accounts of what they do and know how to do. Building an ethnography draws on those individualized resources to begin to make visible how the various aspects of people's work is coordinated. The resources provided by individual accounts can be knitted together to make visible a concerting of activities that might be described as "social organization," "social relations," a "mandated course of action," or some other term that objectifies without displacing the textual presence of the original subjects.

Michael Corman, who wrote an ethnographic account of the work of paramedics in Calgary, Alberta, describes how he moved from his detailed observational practices in the field to an ethnographic account of their work as organized:

> the accounts I provide are not attributed to any one paramedic or observation because I draw on the entirety of my data (all of the observations and interviews I conducted) to construct each composite shift. The accounts given and the characters described should therefore be viewed as composite. ... [T]hese composite accounts and characters allowed me to draw on a diversity of interviews and observations and to represent complex stories about work processes that show 'what I learned' (Campbell and Gregor, 2002, p. 93) as aligned with the analytical goal of this research – to draw attention to some of the complexities of what paramedics do, and how what they do is socially organized, counted, and made institutionally visible. (2017, p. 20)

Corman's ethnography is distinctive because he describes his field observations in detail. This is relatively rare in institutional ethnography; it is a hugely demanding and very time-consuming method (Corman is very good at it). More usual are ethnographies engaging consciously with the institutional relations in which people's work experience is embedded.

> This kind of ethnography takes as its problematic the complex of relations in which the local world is embedded. In this sense, the ethnographic enterprise is not confined to what can be directly observed. Or what informants have directly observed. Rather it seeks to reveal the extended bureaucratic, professional, legislative, and economic, as well as other social relations involved in the local production of events and activities. (Smith, Mykhalovskiy, and Weatherbee, 2006, p. 172)

It is fairly usual for sociologists trained in standard sociology to write into their accounts terms like "social structure," "organizations," and so on that become agents or are used as causes of people's actions. Michael Billig has argued that we "should try to undo the power that nouns seem to have over ... social scientists" and that "we should try to express ourselves in clauses with active verbs" (2013, p. 235). This is not just a matter of style; it is a matter of how we write what we learn from people as an account that assembles the different pieces of what we have learned into a representation that goes beyond any one individual's doings to bring into view a complex of coordinated doings that is ongoing in time. Somehow, we have to draw on what we have and what we are learning from those we talked to in interviews or observed in their work situation to build an account that makes visible how people's work is coordinated without displacing what they do as individuals. Here, then, we could use concepts such as social organization, social relations, mandated courses of action or, as is our focus in chapter 9, the "circular" organizing of institutional language as people's practices. Such concepts direct our ethnographic attention to how what is getting done by given individuals at particular sites and times is entered into and coordinates with sequences of action involving more than one site and time. It is useful to remember here our earlier reference to George Smith's emphasis that a concept such as "social relations" is not to be thought of as a 'thing' but is to be used to "do the looking" (G.W. Smith, 1995, p. 24).

What we are discovering as our ethnographic interest brings people's practices of institutionally authorized words into view is just such a grounding for our ethnography. We are not interested in one-time-only accounts of what people do as such; they will not provide the basis for our ethnographic account – though of course, as our data, our givens, they are its essential grounding. We do, however, need to be able to locate in our observational and/or interview resources just how the institutional dimension of their coordination becomes observable. How can we make that move from the particularities of what actually goes on to a generalized and generalizing account of the workings of ruling or institutional relations? Incorporating people's practices of institutional words into the ethnographic moment of the double dialogue entitles our ethnography to reach beyond particularities to generalizing institutional relations in which texts and the language of institutional texts play a major part.

We have emphasized the significance of texts in coordinating people's institutional forms of action; texts carry language (and, of course, numbers) enabling the standardization of verbal forms across different local sites and times. *Here then is an answer; as words authorized by authorized texts come into play, they hook the ethnographer and the ethnography into the relevant ruling relations.*

Alexander Luria's work (1961, 1976; Luria and Yudovich, 1971) introduced Alison and Dorothy to what Luria calls "verbal generalizing systems." As a by-product of experimental research, Luria noticed that when a child who had no previous experience of a particular object learned from the experimenter's usage – the word naming the object – s/he was also learning to attend selectively to those aspects of the object relevant to its standard use. The word came to organize how the object was perceived. Thus Luria and his associate Yudovich describe how children, in learning to name objects, learn also to focus on the generalized features of named objects (Luria and Yudovich, 1971). These Luria calls verbal generalizing systems: "The word, connected with direct perception of the object ... makes the perception of this object permanent and generalized" (1971, 23). Institutional language, of course, does not refer to specific objects, yet Luria's concept of verbal generalizing systems is suggestive here. What we can begin to look for is how the institutionally authorized language, in a sense, organizes a generalized representation of what is getting done or is produced as people do their assigned work.

Texts authorizing institutional sequences of action are written in a generalizing language; the wording formulates acts, sequences of action, events, agents, and so on in standardizing terms that lack specific referents.

> Institutional work processes are organized by conceptual schemes and distinctive categories. These are the terms in which the accountability of the work is produced, and procedures of accountability provide one of the main ways that various local settings are pulled into translocal relations. (DeVault and McCoy, 2006, p. 37)

People's work, as it is framed in institutional categories, is no longer just the concrete of what is being done; it becomes part of an organized sequence of institutionally mandated action. The standardizing and authorizing languages provide for how variations in process and outcomes of what people do become accountable within institutional governance as parts of a formal sequence coordinated with others.

We are not suggesting that what we might call "institutional language" – the language carried in the replicable texts essential to the very existence of ruling relations – should become a research focus. How the relevant institutional language enters into people's accounts of what they do carries organizing connections with the sequences of others' actions that theirs are hooked up with. The institutional language generalizes and standardizes how actual activities are identified and organized as sequences. Here are some specimens to make this point.

The Grade Appeal

In a journal article (Smith, 2001) about the significance of standardizing texts for the very existence of contemporary institutions as well as large corporations, Dorothy described the result of instituting an official grade appeal procedure in a university sociology department. Before the official establishing of the grade appeal, a student who felt her assignment hadn't been graded as it should have been could seek help from the department chair, who might then get another member of faculty to evaluate the student's work. There is no appeal procedure here; students would have no formal claim to have their grade reviewed nor would a department chair be responsible for following up on the student's initiative. However, once the grade appeal is formally set up, then the department chair has to follow definite procedures.

The formal establishing of a grade appeal procedure (a decision made in a department meeting in which faculty voted) meant that a student could initiate an appeal to the chair in writing; once an appeal had been registered, the chair was responsible for seeing the process through; s/he would have to find a faculty member to do a review; if a change was recommended, the registrar would accept it as the conclusion of an appeal process. The steps identified in the official language of the grade appeal procedure as authorized departmentally accorded the authority to establish appropriately mandated procedures. The actual work of making a grade appeal when taken up by the department chair may not differ greatly from how the chair would proceed when there is no official grade appeal procedure. There are, however, important differences. When there is no official procedure, the chair has no obligation to take up a student's grade appeal in response to the student's request, nor does the chair have any responsibility to follow the sequence through to a conclusion (to make or not make a change).

That we can write of "a grade appeal procedure" is the outcome of an institutionally authorized process that transposes what particular people do into institutional or organizational acts. This is a condition of how we, whether as sociologists or as participants in an organization, are able to speak and write of a grade appeal "procedure" as existing in an ordinary and unexamined way. Note that analysing what has been done in the text's terms also produces different moments or events as steps in a process – the chair and student have agreed on an appraiser and the appraiser has agreed to act – orienting those involved to the next sequence. Different moments or events – the student's consultation with the instructor about her work, for example – become moments in the process by virtue of the text. Coordinating one such moment with others is not direct; neither its effects nor its consequences are relevant to the process without the text that carries the language that frames and recognizes and articulates the different work being done by the participants. The words carried in the text that authorizes the procedure map discrete acts, performed sometimes without direct contact with those involved, into a coordinated sequence. It is in this way that actions and courses of action, analysed and recognized in the language of the authorized text, are coordinated organizationally among people who may not be in direct contact with one another but whose actions, in sequence, depend on what has been done before and orient to what is to follow.

De Montigny's Child Protection Work

Just how the institutional categories in practice organize what people do is very well described in Gerald de Montigny's account (1995n, 2014) of how, in his child protection work, he went about determining whether and how he could make a *case* for removing a child from his or her home (notice here this concept – the very notion of a "case" relies on the existence of the formalized text that organizes the transtemporal continuity of identity to be built upon textually. Of course, today such textual organization is mostly carried electronically). De Montigny was called out when a caretaker reported a commotion involving breaking glass and shouting in one of the apartments. What de Montigny sees, smells, hears when he arrives he treats selectively in terms that fit the categories of child protection law and of the discourse of social work that specifies and supplements it. As he goes through the apartment, he is now looking for *evidence*; he is looking for what will fit the categories of the provincial law on child abuse and neglect (at that time in the 1980s).

Here are some of his observations and how he brings them into relation with his projected institutional course of action – to remove the child temporarily to a group home to be followed up by court action granting custody of the child to a group home. The institutional course of action becomes observable in his account of how he practised its words "in his head."

As I walked into the back bedroom I found an infant … perhaps 10 or 12 months old, lying asleep on top of filthy sheets. … I looked at the child's body to note that she was wearing only a faeces-soiled and urine-soaked diaper. Faeces had dried, and caked her torso and face. I could see that she had been left unattended for several hours without attention to her needs.

Even more disturbing to me was that when I picked her up I saw that the back of her skull was flattened. I assumed that the flattened was not natural. I guessed that it signified the parent's failure to attend to her, and rotating her while sleeping or to pick her up when awake. The flattened skull could be an invaluable piece of evidence before the court. It would serve as a powerful and graphic sign of abnormality resulting from serious neglect. It showed that the child had been left alone lying on her back hour after hour and day after day. ... As I stood in a dimly lit room and breathed in putrid air, I held a groggy child who was beginning to emit frightened cries, yet, my mind was focused on an institutionally defined problem of making a case. I had to establish that this was a child in need of protection. I had to compile sufficient evidence of neglect to make a case, that is, to justify my apprehension, and to be granted custody before the judge in court. (de Montigny, 2014, pp. 176–7)

De Montigny describes vividly his work of fitting the disturbing experiencing of the child's situation and condition into the categories that articulate what he's doing and "thinking" – the words in-skull that organize his present awareness to fit an institutional course of action: he is making a case; he looks for evidence of neglect because removing the child from her home has to be justified before he can apprehend the child into the custody of the child protection services. What we can also see here is how the institutional terms as he practises these words in his head are organizing what he does as an institutionally mandated course of action, going from his work there with the child in her home and to his aim to remove her, and place her in a group home, with sufficient evidence to justify his actions retroactively in court.

Notice that all this organizing of his consciousness is in his head. He can look around the apartment and pick out details to fit the categories of "alcohol abuse" and "neglect." It is his local practice of the words that *organize* his present awareness in orienting to what he will aim at doing and achieving within the institutional settings. The organizing done with words in his head is relating him to an institutionally defined course of action. His word-organized work is becoming the opening moments of the mandated course of action that will conclude with the court process and securing custody of the child and her final removal from her home. It is the institutional words that organize what de Montigny was doing in one place with subsequent moments in an institutionally recognizable sequence.

Alison's Observation of "Institution Talk"

Alison has described particular kinds of talk as "institution talk," typically spoken in the context of describing an institutional course of action. It may be only a phrase, or a category of identification. For example, when talking to teachers or school administrators, Alison sometimes found them using terms that were not intelligible to her. One of the phrases they used was "my Level 2s and 3s." For example, if a teacher was talking about her curricular planning, she might mention that her curricular goals and objectives for the year are different from other years. Perhaps, she said, she has more Level 2s in her classroom this year. When teachers described their students in terms of achievement levels, they were "talking" the institution talk. What Alison learned, from talking with the teachers and exploring the relevant websites, was how this language was integral to the institutional designing of province-wide student tests introduced into Ontario in 1996. Once each year in Ontario, students in Grades 3, 6, and 10 take the Education Quality and Accountability Office (EQAO) tests. The tests are given late in the school year, and the results are not available until the following year.

The tests are not only an individual record of achievement; they are also the basis on which schools are evaluated, and as well form the basis for individual teachers' curricular planning. What is the distribution of students among the four achievement levels? What are the school's and teacher's achievement objectives and goals for the year? How will students meet those? In the fall, student achievement levels from the previous year are given to the teacher. Her or his curricular planning will reflect how many Level 1, Level 2, Level 3, or Level 4 students will be in the classroom. Level 3 and 4 students are considered not to have met provincial achievement standards. School achievement scores are ranked by EQAO and the Ministry of Education each year. Typically, the school, and therefore the teacher's curricular emphasis, will be on the high-scoring Level 2s and low-scoring Level 3s because these students' scores are the most friable.

Had a serious ethnography been undertaken of this use of phrases, we'd have needed to discover how the word "levels" is used by the teachers in their everyday talk about their classrooms; how it enters into their actual classroom work and organizes their relations with their students. So too, exploring these language practices can bring into view how they organize the work of students and teachers in the relevant grades as preparation for the tests. This iterative language use refers to aspects of how people's work is coordinated that is ordinary and familiar to them but not to those, like Alison, who are not directly involved.

We note, in this context, that in interviews, respondents in their use of "institution talk" may take for granted that we know what they are talking about – or if in fact you are also someone who participates in the same institutional discourse and speaks the language, you may take for granted that you know what they are talking about. But if in an interview your respondent has used the terminology and if you had assumed you knew what s/he is talking about, you may find when you look at the transcript of the interview that there is no actual information about what has been going on and what was being referred to. It will matter for your ethnography to explore terms like "levels" to find the ruling relations your respondent was speaking about – even if you think you know what such institutional talk means.

Conclusion

In these three specimens, we can see how institutional language carried in institutional texts organizes people's work as institutionally mandated sequences. Attending to the language as it comes into play in the observations we make or the interviews connecting us with those who are doing the work shows us how the particularities of any actual work done by people can be discovered as they participate, through local language practices, in sequences that, in a sense, are reproduced in multiple instances. These sequences are never actually the same, but the institutional organization is present in terms that tie them to the textually authorized procedures. From time to time we have used words such as "organize" to suggest something of how the verbal mandating of sequences of action coordinate people's doings. We have also made it clear that we do not want to get hung up on notions such as "social organization," even though they may seem entirely appropriate when we have brought our institutional ethnography to the point where institutional standardization is fully visible in particular people's doings. But now we are making a shift. We're no longer just recognizing how institutionally named "objects" are built out of selected aspects of actualities encoded as "textual realities"; we are now beginning to make observable how *institutional courses of action are vested in words* that, as they are practised, name the particularities of what people are doing as the actions, outcomes, and so on identified in the authorizing texts. In writing the ethnography, however, the institutional language on its own should not become a discrete topic. We are not recommending a focus on language that separates it from what people are or have been getting done, but we can see in these specimens how the language of the institutional texts, the Ontario "bawdy-house" law for example or de Montigny's account of how the professional language of social work, once he had internalized it, organizes work. Attending to respondents' use of the relevant institutional language helps the ethnographic researcher to make visible an important dimension of institutional coordination.

The following chapters will bring into view some of the discoveries institutional ethnographers have made in the course of developing ethnographies. In all these ethnographies we will be able to recognize how the language carried in the relevant texts organizes people's work as articulated to what others have done or will do. We will also be able to learn more about some of the distinctive ways in which institutional language brings into play a standardization of people's doings, even though, of course, in actual practice, what is done is always in and of an ongoing world and never exactly the same at another moment in time.

Chapter Eight

Exploring Ruling Relations

When we organize our ethnographic projects, we are at odds with standard sociology. Like the IE explorers of the mountain range in chapter 1, we start off from our own particular position and interests – what we care about. This does not mean beginning in an autobiographical mode, though it may be useful to describe how your research interest came out of your own everyday life – as Alison and Dorothy did when they drew on their experiences as single parents in developing their research into the work mothers do for schools. Rather, it does mean that we are coming from somewhere, that we care about the issues we explore, and that we start off from what we share with others. An institutional ethnography project that begins without any such direction runs into the problem of the real world; it's messy; it doesn't have a direction as such. Previously, Dorothy described the difficulty of deciding what was important to her research in the California state mental health hospital where she did her doctoral research. Miles away from that description, we find a similar problem arising for the researcher. Think again of going to the grocery store and imagining all the connections you are making, not only with the organization of the store, the corporation that owns and manages it, but also the many sources of the food it is selling, how the packaging is manufactured, and so on. If we can't pick up a theory to tell us what will be relevant, what are we to do?

The institutional ethnography project is one of discovering; the researcher does not know exactly where the research will take him or her. Hence, it is important to have a sense of what is relevant to the concerns that drive the research. We have come to use the term "standpoint" for this positioning of the research. Let us be clear: the notion of standpoint should not be treated as if it identifies an entity of some kind. Again, it is not theory, and you certainly do not have to use the term if it you find it tiresome. Standpoint is to be understood as a way of directing attention to the starting place of the inquiry. Research direction is given by working from a basis in people's experience, perhaps the researcher's own. This is the place from which the research can begin to look for how people's experience of their everyday world is to be opened up and explicated as it intersects with social relations that reach beyond the immediacy of their experience. In the first and introductory chapter of this book, we drew on what might be described as the problematic developed by Marx and Engels for the future of their work together. People always start from themselves yet there are relations existing independently of individuals that overpower their lives. Though IE's focus is not on relations that are primarily coordinated by money, we also begin with actual people and open up, as a research problematic, the textually mediated relations that stand over against us and overpower our lives. Institutional ethnography's research problematic opens up where problems for people can be located in relevant aspects of the ruling relations. Contrary to the view that the objectivity of research requires the researcher to displace any particular interests in the research outcome, an institutional ethnography works from the interests and concerns of actual people. The researcher's care and commitment to accuracy and exactitude is responsive to the importance of being able to tell people how things are actually being put together so that they can recognize how they are entered into the actualities of their experience.

The choice of where to start and what to develop as the problematic of an institutional ethnography is always something that the researcher cares about and may indeed be actively involved with. The issue or problem is likely not already formulated; indeed, a pre-existing formulation is likely to deflect the project from discovering how and where institutional relations actually enter into, organize, and are giving trouble to people as they participate in them. In developing a research direction, it is useful to open up those aspects of people's experience of intersections with ruling relations that can be identified as contributing to the problem or problems that awakened concern. One example is ours, Alison's and Dorothy's, referred to above. We talked with each other on our Sunday hikes in the Toronto ravines about the problems we were experiencing with our children's schooling. Out of our discussions, Alison's dissertation research developed. She wrote her doctoral thesis on the ideology of single parenthood and the kind of blaming of single-parent families for all kinds of problems in school board settings in Toronto. After Alison completed her dissertation, we decided we would apply for research funding to learn something about what it was that made "non-defective" families so important to schools. Our problematic in this case came out of our own experience; we developed it further by interviewing each other about the work, in the generous sense, that goes into getting children to and from school, seeing to their meals, bedtimes, and reading to them as well as any support for their schoolwork that was to be done. We went on to interview a small number of women from two school districts, one with a predominantly professional-middle-class population and the other a low-income one. But notice, we were not interested just in what the mothers were doing as so many who have studied them have been; we were interested in how the work they did and how they did it *coordinated with the schools' work*, and so we also interviewed the principals, vice-principals, and teachers and a couple of assistant superintendents at the school board level. *Our problematic was a starting place and a direction in which to take our research.* From that starting place, that standpoint, and given that direction, we went on to learn what we could about the dovetailing of the work that mothers do for schooling and the ways in which the school operates given the different conditions under which mothering work was done in the two school districts.

Our research did not focus explicitly on how ruling relations organized what we were discovering. But those relations were there in how the school day was regulated to complement mothers' work with the school-day schedule. As we will see, the aspects of ruling that are brought into view differ in the researches described below. Their visibility depends on the standpoint that the ethnographer works from and with. This is not bias. Institutional ethnography works reflexively; there is no other way for inquiry to proceed except from where the explorer is located. As with all research, the researcher's interest guides their science. Through experience, observation, reading, and adhering to and questioning proven methods of gathering data, the researcher pulls together a topic to be investigated. What s/he learns is grounded scrupulously in what is actually going on among people. But the view that emerges is oriented by what we are identifying, for the purposes of this discussion, as the problematic of their research.

In this chapter we examine three major institutional ethnographic enterprises. All four researchers were fully familiar with institutional ethnography as an approach, though George Smith's research work was done before Tim Diamond and Dorothy, sitting on a beach in southern California, came up with that name. We are aiming to learn from these four ethnographers how they framed the direction of their research, what they investigated, and how what we're calling the "ruling relations" entered into and organized the everyday world that they explored. The ethnographic research projects they undertake are not hiding under a theoretical carapace. They are not case studies. Rather, the ethnographic projects are explorations oriented by the researcher's interests and experience. They are concerned with what is happening and how it is organized within relations that reach across local experience. Though they do not generalize in the traditional sociological sense, making statements that apply across multiple settings, they are dimensions of how the generalizing relations of ruling work in the local practices in which they come into action.

The first of these projects was undertaken by George Smith arising out of his participation in gay activist organizing in the Toronto gay community of the 1980s and 1990s; the second is Gerald de Montigny's account of how he entered into, learned, and practised what he called the professional discourse of social work; and the third is Janet Rankin and Marie Campbell's account of the managerial reorganization of hospital nurses' work in British Columbia.

George Smith's Research Problematics

George Smith was a gay activist from the 1980s until his death from AIDS in 1994. He had taken up the approach that is now known as institutional ethnography because it was relevant to the gay experience and the developing gay activism of the time. He saw Dorothy's new social science as an approach enabling a scientifically grounded knowledge of the actual workings of translocal social relations.

Smith had worked in Vancouver with Dorothy in Women's Research Centre projects, bringing together women to share their experiences of oppressions, helping them clarify shared problems, and then making visible the ruling relations implicit in their stories as a basis for organizing for change (these Women's Research Centre projects were where IE originated). When Smith moved to Toronto to work towards his doctorate at the Ontario Institute for Studies in Education, he became part of the gay community there and participated in the gay activism of the time. He was in Dorothy's program in what was then known as the "social organization of knowledge" and worked with her as a research associate. His brilliant understanding and creative development of what came to be known as institutional ethnography made exceptional advances as he brought it into relation with his gay activist concerns.

Smith pursued three research projects (he died of AIDS before the last was concluded) all of which worked from problematics framed by his gay activist concerns. He formulated the conception of "activist as ethnographer" (1990) when gay activists in Toronto were raising major issues about charges brought against gay men engaged in sexual activity in bathhouses raided by the police. Gay activists represented the problem with the police as one of police homophobia. Smith took a very different view. Police practices were authorized within a regime beyond the scope of individual or collective attitudes.

> Beginning with the experience of having our sexual lives regulated by the authorities, we decided to render this opaque feature of our everyday world problematic. We used the notion of "problematic" to set out a form of inquiry that, starting from the position of individuals in the everyday world, is directed at illuminating how their world is shaped and determined by social processes that go beyond it – specifically in our case, of course, the work of the police in regulating sex. (G.W. Smith 1990, p. 168)

Smith did research that made visible the work of undercover police in writing a report based on observations of the sexual activity going on in a bathhouse. The report was carefully designed to describe behaviour that could be fitted to the categories of Ontario's "bawdy-house" law (see the section on "textual reality" in chapter 9) thus providing the basis on which charges could be brought against the men found in the bathhouses when they were raided.

The problematic of Smith's (1995) second line of research arose out of his own experience, as well as those of other gay men, of the problems of getting medical treatment for AIDS. AIDS had been identified with gay sexuality in public discourse and hence became of special concern for gay activists. At that time there was no cure but there were medications that could help with the problems of living with AIDS. Smith's research problematic was developed in relation to his activism with the organization AIDS ACTION NOW!. His concern was the Ontario government's lack of support in health care policies and administration for medical treatment that might alleviate and improve the health of people with AIDS. Here was the problematic of the research he undertook.

> [I]t was the frustration over the lack of experimental treatments for people living with AIDS that led, first, to the investigation of government activities, and, second, to the discovery that government intervention in the epidemic was first and forever grounded in public health legislation. With the discovery that the government had no legislative mandate to provide new, experimental treatment for individuals, public health relations came into view ... as the preoccupation of the politico-administrative regime managing the epidemic. It was this preoccupation that resulted in the government being concerned almost entirely for the uninfected and about the spread of the disease, on the one side, and on the other, doing precious

little for those who were already infected, sick, or dying – apart, of course, for some financial support for palliative care. (1995, pp. 26–7)

The study's most important finding about the management of the AIDS epidemic, from the standpoint of people living with AIDS or HIV infection, was the lack of an infrastructure to manage the delivery of new, experimental treatments. These findings have directed the work of AIDS ACTION NOW! in designing and in putting in place just such an infrastructure (G.W. Smith, 1990, p. 630).

Both research projects were oriented to Smith's participation in gay activist organizations. He was interested in developing workable and appropriate activist objectives based not on ideology, but on a knowledge of just how the problem on which the activists were focused became operative within the relevant ruling relations.

> The constant political confrontation between the Right to Privacy, AIDS ACTION NOW! and its respective, politico-administrative *regime* operated … to prioritize the sites of investigative work. Political forays, often as it had so far developed, continued to orient the collection and examination of the data from the standpoint of the problematic. … The success of our political strategies – as in the proof of the pudding is in the eating – was a measure of the competency of the analysis in organizing effective political interventions. (1990, p. 644)

Smith's investigations contributed to his own active role in raising issues as well as to the activism of the movement in which he participated. His main aim was to contribute directly to activism in the region opened as the problematic of his research. His scholarly publications only partially cover the extent of his research. His 1995 account of his AIDS ACTION NOW! research project refers to substantial ethnographic research but unfortunately it has gone missing; he was probably still in the process of writing it when he died. When Dorothy, who was his literary executor, arrived in Vancouver, where he had done much of his writing, she learned that his computer had been wiped because his brother needed it.

In the last stage of Smith's life, he was developing, with Eric Mykhalovskiy and Douglas Weatherbee, a research project (G.W. Smith et al., 2006) that came out of his own experience of the work involved in coordinating the services of different public services – health, welfare, and so on – to meet the needs of people living, as he was, with HIV/AIDS. This was no longer research with a problematic grounded in issues of exclusively gay men. Nor did it emerge out of Smith's own activist activity. Rather, it was grounded in Smith's experience as someone living with AIDS and doing the work of keeping going, getting medical care, drawing on welfare resources, and so on.

> For the most part, the main business of AIDS is addressed from the standpoint of health care and social services systems. ... This study takes a different approach. It begins from the standpoint of those who are HIV or have AIDS: it examines the social services from their standpoint. (G.W. Smith et al., 2006, p. 167)

What is distinctive about the project was that it opened up the work that people with AIDS and those supporting them were doing to keep going.

> We call this the "lifework" of people because it is critical to their efforts to extend their lives. (G.W. Smith et al., 2006, p. 167)

It explored PWA's (People With AIDS) experience of working with the health care system as well as the social services they came to depend on when they were no longer employed. In contrast with research approaches examining people who were HIV-positive or had AIDS from the institutional perspective, the research undertaken by Smith, Mykhalovskiy, and Weatherbee aimed to learn from people's own experience of coordinating their "lifework" with the organization of the social services.

Overall, in his research and thinking, Smith develops problematics arising from contradictions between the experience and concerns of people and the social relations of the governing regime as they are imposed upon them. Here he formulates a general conception of an organizing problematic as grounded in

> an everyday feature of our society, ... [namely,] how these various institutional sites of regulation and control are merged together to create ... a politico-administrative regime. ... [T]he notion of a politico-administrative regime operates as an heuristic device for investigating empirically how ruling works, how the lives of people are regulated and governed by institutions and individuals vested with authority. (G.W. Smith, 1990, p. 637)

Gerald de Montigny's Discovery of the Powers of Institutional Discourse

Institutional discourse is not de Montigny's term; we have introduced it simply to preserve the connection between his work and the concepts presented here as the working orientation of an institutional ethnography. As in the time of George Smith's research, the term "institutional ethnography" had not yet been established but de Montigny is clearly working within the same conceptual frame as had been worked out by graduate students with Dorothy Smith at the Ontario Institute for Studies in Education (OISE) (see Campbell and Manicom, 1995). The ethnographic focus of his study of social working is de Montigny's experience of learning and practising the professional discourse of social work as he first discovered it when he was in training as a social worker and then in his practice as a child protection worker.

The problematic organizing de Montigny's is based on his own experience of the deep contradictions between his view of the world as a young working-class man and that of the social work profession that he was required to impose on his consciousness as he trained to be a social worker. He grew up in a working-class family; his work experience before he went to university was characteristic of the working-class world. His book (based on his doctoral dissertation) explores ethnographically the difficulties he experienced both in learning the proper practice of social work's professional discourse as a student and in how that discourse organized his professional practice as a social worker. As an undergraduate at the University of British Columbia (UBC), he confronted the problem of learning a new and middle-class way of thinking and seeing the world. But beyond that was what he encountered when he entered a master's degree program in social work at the University of Toronto. He experienced a deep disjuncture between the world that he knew, on the one hand, as a worker and understood in terms of the relations of class and, on the other, what he was required to learn as a text-grounded discourse that imposed its distinctive categories as requirements of professional practice.

> As a manual labourer I obeyed and served others, minded my place, and worked physically. As a professional, I ordered and directed others, assumed responsibility, and worked mentally. ... How do people produce the specific professional consciousness required to manage their place and their work as social workers within an institutional apparatus?
>
> I came from another place, another class, and another reality, which made being a social worker difficult. ... From my standpoint, I found it difficult believing that social services organizations were about helping, fairness, equity, equality, and human dignity. Having stood in line for unemployment insurance, having entered a welfare office needing money, having the problem of making 'ends meet' on pogie, I could not accept professional versions of organizational beneficence. Nor could I accept the

clinical reduction of social problems to issues of personality or individual maladjustment. (de Montigny, 1995a, p. 40)

The contradiction between de Montigny's experience growing up in a working-class family and the forms of organizing thought and consciousness that he had to adopt as he became a social worker is central to his ethnography. In his practice as a social worker, he saw that issues, such as those of unemployment and poverty, had no presence in social work's professional discourse. Throughout his ethnography, he is explicating, *as specific practices*, how the textual discourse of social work enters into and organizes the local practices of his professional work, particularly in his specialty area of child protection. Throughout his account of the distinctive properties of social work professional discourse, he brings into view how it imposes a version of a world: the problems of individuals are represented in categories that pathologize or criminalize them and that legitimate such acts as removing a child from its family. The actual connections between their situations and societal problems such as poverty or unemployment have no presence in that textually organized discourse.

De Montigny goes on from the general exploration of the text-grounded discourse of professional social work to open up in greater detail his own experiences of doing child protection work. He examines how what he does and had to do was organized discursively. His daily work involved practices of translating what he directly experienced and felt in the local settings (in which he encountered the people he had to deal with) into the discursive categories enabling the legislatively mandated course of action to be imposed on them.

When I left the office, I moved towards worlds where people smash their fist through windows, where razor blades course across wrists, and where people hurt others and hurt themselves. These are worlds where rage is expressed, tempers explode, threats are made against people's lives, people scream, lash out, and move in ways that are not acceptable in the office. When I left the physical space of the office, my movement was in one sense a break with the office. In another sense, I was an agent of the office. ... When I stood at the door of the client's home I was embodied and vulnerable. As I sat at my desk and wrote, the writing effected a transformation. As the author of reports and documents on file, I assumed an Archimedean standpoint to gaze back on to my practice and the lives of my clients. My writing activities produced an 'objectifying gaze' ... through which sensations, movements, confusion and chaos were rewritten into discursively coherent patterns. (de Montigny, 1995a, p. 170)

De Montigny's experiential account of his conflicted consciousness brings into view some of the very distinctive aspects of what we might here call institutional discourse (he used the concept of ideology). He identified the distinctive language of social work as he learned and came to use it in his professional work as deeply in contradiction with what he knew as a working-class man. He emphasizes in his ethnography the interchange between texts as pre-existing his actions, as being produced through the actions of social workers, and as being read by social workers. But these discourses are not just about social work; they are institutional actions that impinge on and shape the lives of social work clients.

Of course, the particulars of the categories that come into play in his practice are those of social work discourse of the period in which he wrote – the late 1980s. Much has changed since then, particularly the technology of texts. When he was writing his ethnography of his practice as a social worker, records were still being kept by writing on paper which were transformed into typed documents by secretaries. The use of computers for writing and of course the development of electronic modes of coding and recording information was still to come and no doubt has changed the everyday practice of social work in contemporary Canada. Also, there have likely been changes in the legislation that have had to be built into the professional discourse. However, the forms of dominance through institutional language that de Montigny describes are still operating. And indeed when we think of what we may be learning from his remarkable ethnography, we can see that what is added to our view of the ruling relations by his investigation is a vivid understanding of just how institutional language organizes the everyday practices of people in a profession.

Rankin and Campbell's Problematic

Over the last fifty years of nursing care, Canadian hospitals have been subjected to increasingly intensive forms of managing that standardize the care to be provided by imposing systems of patient classification, or by classifying the patients' needs for nursing care. Janet Rankin and Marie Campbell's study, *Managing to Nurse: Inside Canada's Health Care Reform* (2006), focuses on how nurses' practical hospital work is being reorganized by the introduction of the standardizations of management aimed at the cost-efficiency of hospital functioning (see also Rankin 1998, 2001). Both Rankin and Campbell had trained and worked as professional nurses. When they undertook the research reported in their book, both had faculty positions in academic settings. Both had also taken up sociology, using institutional ethnography as their approach. They had become aware of significant changes in Canadian hospitals involving the introduction of new managerial approaches combined with electronic technologies. Both Rankin's and Campbell's own knowledge as nurses, as well as what they learned as academics from their contacts in the field, had made explicit for them that it is nurses' work that "holds a clinical environment together, making it run smoothly, creating it as a space where health caring activity can proceed" (Rankin and Campbell, 2006, p. 4). This vital work appears only as "background ... in accounts of [nurses] work" (Rankin and Campbell, 2006, p. 4); its importance as creating the conditions for the clinical work with patients is not recognized. Rankin and Campbell's ethnographic exploration takes up and learns from nurses' experiences of how new managerial changes are entering into nurses' work at the front line of patient care where they are holding the clinical environment together:

> In the restructured health care system, the provision of services is coordinated textually. The new methods, the accounting logic, and its managerial implementation require that the patients, nurses, and nursing be reformulated, calculated, and enumerated. The management of planning and resource allocation, programs of therapeutic interventions, and process and outcome monitoring take place on the basis of this textual representation; that is, they are worked up and worked on as virtual realities. (2006, p. 15)

Rankin and Campbell make visible

> from the standpoint of nurses, how admission, discharge, and transfer (ADT, that is, Admit-Discharge-Transfer) software works as a technology of governance within the hospital. Hospitals must account for and manage carefully all the costs of providing hospital care, including the use of buildings and bed capacity – and the latter is where ADT becomes important. (2006, p. 45)

Rankin's experience doing participant observation as a nurse in practice is vividly told. She describes a particular work experience in which the ADT comes into play in the practical organization of the nurses' work. Her account makes visible just how the new managerial technologies are implemented by the responsible nurse even when they are at odds with professional principles of patient care. Rankin was working with Nurse Linda to prepare Ms Shoulder for discharge. Ms Shoulder was recovering from surgery on her shoulder, which was still immobilized with a specialized application. She was due for discharge. Waiting for her bed was Ms Leg Wound, who was due for surgery. Janet could see that Ms Shoulder needed considerable help with just getting dressed and getting to the toilet; she was also experiencing nausea and needed some careful instruction about how to care for her shoulder immobilizer when she was at home. Nurse Linda, however, had to speed up the process of discharge. Rather than consulting a physician to get an appropriate prescription, she gave Ms Shoulder a handy anti-nausea medication that did not require a prescription. And rather than allowing her to rest longer in bed, the process of getting her up and out was speeded up: Nurse Linda had to give her instructions for home care very fast, without having time to ensure that Ms Shoulder fully understood them. Rankin does not suggest that Nurse Linda was incompetent, rather that she was under pressure dealing with the problems of two patients at the same time. As she was preparing Ms Shoulder for discharge, Nurse Linda was also preparing Ms Leg Wound for surgery and making sure that Ms Shoulder's bed would be available when Ms Leg Wound had to be accommodated.

> The constant overlap of patients shapes the 'speeded up' work processes of nurses who are always, nevertheless, irremediably grounded in the embodied actualities of their daily/nightly work. Patients have bodies and they need real beds. When new patients arrive, they require nursing attention, even if they do not appear in a nurse's assignment. And, besides taking care of the extra bodies, the overlap that the use of fictitious beds creates is consequential for nurses in another way. It is up to nurses to see that the virtual bed to which the new patient is assigned is actually available when the patient needs it. This accounts for nurse Linda 'taking shortcuts' when caring for Ms. Shoulder. It explains why she would have given her discharge instructions when Ms. Shoulder was in pain, and it explains why she put aside Ms. Shoulder's nausea and discomfort and hurried her out of the hospital. Nurse Linda and her colleagues have learned to adapt their nursing care to the dictates of the hospital's overriding concern about excessive spare bed capacity. This is how the ADT system organizes and even restructures nurses' work. (Rankin and Campbell, 2006, p. 52–3)

Other computer technologies standardize "clinical pathways" and "care-type." Patients with certain diagnoses can be assigned clinical pathways that establish a specific treatment regime, including a standardized timing of discharge. The case-type technology identifies patients whose condition makes them the inappropriate occupants of beds in acute care; "[t]he designation also triggers a differentiated and reduced nursing regimen for these patients" (2006, p. 66). Rankin and Campbell point out that these are "virtual realities" that subordinate what nurses know through their professionally guided direct knowledge of patients as individuals and "thereby restructures nurses' judgment and action" (Rankin and Campbell, 2006, p. 66).

The two speech genres (styles of language use) (Bakhtin, 1986), one of professional nursing and the other managerial, are often contradictory. For example, in some of her interviews, Rankin discovered different uses of the notion of "quality of care." In one, a nurse was critical of the "quality of care" when a patient who'd returned home after gynecological surgery was discovered to still have her vaginal packing in place. In another, when she was interviewing one of the hospital's directors, Rankin heard a different usage of "quality of care." For the nursing manager, the "quality of nursing care" referred to "[a] unit's performance statistics over a six-month period. ... It was her job to make sure that patients were cared for within the statistical guidelines that were being established as benchmarks across the region and further afield" (Rankin and Campbell, 2006, p. 141).

Regardless of the intentions of those who created the standardizing management concepts used in contemporary nursing, different usages are not unusual. Another wobbly concept is "efficiency." For nurses, being efficient has meant organizing the work to be done effectively in attending to patients' individual needs. "Efficiency" in managerial terms refers to the hospital's cost-saving measures and being efficient means working with the constraints of the computer technology designed to advance it.

> The social life of nursing practice is being restructured. Within the historicity of that social restructuring, accomplished through the implementation of the new public management's efficiency practices, nursing discourse is also being restructured. A new speech genre is evolving. In this new speech genre, hospital and nursing managers adopt terms from the conceptual jurisdiction of the traditional professional nursing genre, and nurses adopt terms from the genre of hospital management. (Rankin and Campbell, 2006, p. 161)

What We Can Learn

We can see very clearly in these accounts how the concerns of the researchers organize the direction of research. George Smith's first research focused on the bathhouse raids makes visible for gay activists just how it became possible for the city attorney to bring charges against the owner, the manager, and those "found in" the bathhouse. Sadly, because of his early death from AIDS, what Smith was learning about the absence of public health support for people suffering with HIV/AIDS was never fully written up into a publication, nor was he able to fully develop his explorations with Eric Mykhaloskiy and Douglas Wetherbee of how it was actually those caring for themselves who were coordinating social and health care services.

De Montigny brings into view the class orientation built into the social work discourse of his professional training and practice, both in the process of reorienting his consciousness and awareness in the course of his professional training, and then in how it organized his professional practice. It is a highly original investigation of a professional discourse because it is brought into play in the everyday work and consciousness of a professional. As a method of researching, de Montigny's study provides a model of how the researcher's own experience can be drawn on as a source of data. Of course, he references texts as sources, but his primary data is his own experiences of learning and practising professional social work discourse.

Rankin and Campbell create a fascinating and conclusive account of how new practices of management imposed on a hospital in British Columbia reorganize the front-line of nurses' care of patients. Their study also introduces a new dimension of ethnography developed from the problematic of their concerns. They were discovering from the standpoint of nurses' everyday work how new managerial technologies and forms of accountability change the demands of their front-line work; they also open up, without actually exploring, a whole dimension of new managerial practices being introduced into public services. This was a region later taken up in Alison's and Dorothy's workshop-originating collection of studies exploring the reorganization of various public services in Canada – *Under New Public Management: Institutional Ethnographies of Changing Front-line Work* (Griffith and Smith, 2014).

Chapter Nine

Institutional Circuits: From Actual to Textual

In this chapter, we turn to concepts that institutional ethnographers have come to see as useful in opening up key aspects of how complex relations, mediated by institutional language vested in texts, are co-ordinated as sequences of action. We have drawn together here those concepts that trace circuits going from some actuality of people's experience to institutionally mandated sequences of action in which institutional language is used to manage people's work. The institutional ethnographies described in what follows bring into view "circularities" knitting actualities into the institutional language organizing people's ongoing doings. The chapter begins with the early discovery within institutional ethnography of "ideological circles," then moves to discoveries of how the work of producing textual representations articulates to institutional courses of action, and finally takes up the notion of institutional circuits with two examples for exploring changing forms of management, such as those introduced in our account of Rankin and Campbell's *Managing to Nurse*.

Ideological Circles

The concept of an "ideological circle" was perhaps the earliest discovery of the distinctive ways in which institutional texts and the language they carry coordinate sequences of action (Smith, 1974). The concept was developed originally from Marx and Engels's critique of "German ideology" (Marx and Engels, 1976; see also Smith, 2004). They showed how the reasoning of those they called "German ideologists" went from an ordinary actuality to an abstract conceptualization, which was then held to generate the original actuality as described. Ideological circles begin with a concept or theory that is used in creating accounts to treat original actualities selectively to become its expressions or effects (Marx and

Figure 4. The ideological circle

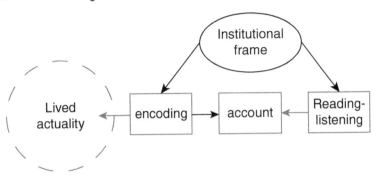

Engels, 1976, p. 508). The notion of an ideological circle locates a sequence of action going from the concepts or theories of a discourse to picking out those aspects of what is or has been going on to develop an account to be understood in terms of the concept or theory used to organize it. The circle is a sequence. It begins as someone deploys a concept from an institutional discourse in attending selectively to some aspect of actualities that has become his or her focus. That person then produces, writes, or speaks, or otherwise inscribes an account that can be read or heard in terms of the same concept or theory that organized the process of selecting from local actualities. What was originally going on or was there has no presence in the account that is there to be understood and taken up.

Ideological circles during an inquiry are something to look for in explicating how a given sequence of action is organized institutionally. The concept is useful in making visible the institutional or discursive frames organizing how actualities are selectively interpreted. Jean Louis Deveau (2014) has written an ethnographic account using the concept of an ideological circle to make visible his own experience of how a physical problem he had that affected his work situation became invisible when he had to use the framework of federal government disability categories in making a formal complaint. He deploys the concept of the ideological circle to show both to himself and to his readers just how the actualities of his disability, and indeed those of people with disabilities in general, disappear as they become represented officially by medically modelled diagnostic categories. He describes how he himself practised the ideological circle that trapped his actual experience of his disability situation into the official categories required in making an official complaint about his changed work situation. His practical problems and needs disappear in the terms required for the official complaint.

Deveau asks us to dismiss the understanding of disability as a bodily inadequacy and to replace it with what those who are actually living with everyday problems in their bodily functioning experience. As an outcome of renovations being made at his workplace, Deveau discovered himself trapped in an ideological circle organized by what he calls the "medical model," that is, the treatment of disability as a "personal defect" identified with specific categories that take on the capacity of causal agents. His account of his practising of an ideological circle begins with the problems he experienced when his office was retrofitted with state-of-the-art air ventilation and air conditioning. Deveau needs office space with a window that can be opened so he does not become ill. After the building renovations, he could not find an office with an "operable" window and hence he kept getting sick. When he complained about the situation he was experiencing, using the framework of the Workplace Accommodation Policy, he found himself caught up in an ideological circle that precluded recognition of his ordinary experience of what had made him sick in the workplace, namely the lack of a window he could open. His lived experience of his disability in this new situation was displaced by the official definitions. His problem became defined in terms of the federal government's established generalizing categories of "disability." The category "environmental sensitivity" was the one that applied to his situation, a categorization that allowed for no recognition of the ordinary practicalities of the real-life situations he experienced. "My 'environmental sensitivity' became my blazon, an attribute which set me apart from my other colleagues at work, an attribute that made me feel like I was a freak" (2014, p. 320).

Here he clarifies some of the distinctive properties of institutional concepts and how they operate within an ideological circle, drawing on his own experience as a person with a specific disabling condition:

At Step 1, my experiential condition is exposed as raw material for an ideological transformation. Basically, I became sick because I did not have access to an operable window. Since there are no windows or Deveaus in our Workplace Accommodation Policy (henceforth referred to as the policy), the connective to both was severed, at Step 2, after I activated the policy. ... I as subject and the link I have with an operable window become nominalized as environmental sensitivity, 'an abstract noun capable of functioning as an agent.' ... What this means is that agency has been transferred from I, as subject, to the concept known as environmental sensitivity, presented in Part 4 of our policy as follows: 'Installation of air filters to restrict or limit respiratory or skin irritants (environmental sensitivities).' The nominalized form thus assumes the function of grammatical subject which can then enter, as Smith… writes, 'into relations independently of the explicit presence of the subject or subjects to whose actions it refers.' (Deveau, 2014, p. 9)

Deveau's analysis is complex and elegant and goes much beyond what we have room for here – we recommend you read it – but this abbreviated account does bring into view how the textually mediated words of institutional discourses, as people take them up and practise them, coordinate what they do or what's going on for them with ongoing sequences of institutional action. Ideological circles are thus to be understood as aspects of organizing institutional sequences of action – in Deveau's case, making a formal complaint in search of appropriate modifications of his workplace. In becoming active in making the complaint, he discovers that his actual situation can have no official recognition. What he actually experiences and needs in practice disappears in the formal categorization of his disability as a condition of "environmental sensitivity." "Environmental sensitivity" now *stands in as the cause of his problem*, rather than the lack of a window that he can open. The formal "diagnostic" category is authorized; it establishes official recognition of his disability; at the same time, what is actually going on for him in his workplace situation cannot be addressed. In making a formal complaint, he became active in the ideological circle that entrapped him.

In moving to explore the topic of "textual realities," we will be taking this circular sequence further in bringing into view how organized work sequences produce textual representations that become the "reality" enabling institutionally mandated courses of action.

Textual Realities

While reading linguistic studies, Dorothy encountered the work of Hans-Jörg Schmid (2000), who introduced her to a type of noun that lacks specific content – for example, "thing," "fact," "case," "reason," and so on. Such nouns can be seen as waiting to be filled. Schmid calls them "shells." Schmid's treatment of shells and how they are filled is confined to sentence structures or sequences, but his account suggested an analogy for how the categories of the "boss texts" of institutional discourse are also waiting to be filled with substance extracted from the actualities of people's lives and doings. The contents are not the original actualities, but rather *representations* constructed to fit the shells of institutional discourse.

The term "textual realities" as we use it here brings into view the work people do creating textual representations that are brought into play in institutionally organized courses of action. The institutional language of authoritative or "boss" texts activated in various settings makes it possible to generalize representations across multiple particular settings. The local particularities of what's happening among people disappear as they deploy the institutional language in producing its representation. Somehow, work has to be done to select what can become treated as what is or has been or will be *there* if institutional sequences of action are to proceed. What we are opening up here is work done to bring the real world into the scope of institutional forms of action.

There are what we can call "governing" or "boss" texts – for example, theories, laws, procedures, policies, rules, regulations, and so on – that manage how actualities are selectively attended to in constructing textual representations, giving concrete substance in the actual situations of people's ongoing work of delivering the everyday reality of the ruling relations. The process is circular, very much the same as the "ideological circle" (see Figure 4). A boss text is set up. Inscription, that is, the work of selecting from actualities to make a textual reality, is governed by the relevant boss text. A textual reality has been created. Deveau's real-life need for a window that can be opened so that he does not get sick has become an "environmental sensitivity." Once an account of an actuality articulated to a given institutional course of action has been produced, it can be interpreted and handled for action within the relevant institution's scope. In Deveau's case, the official diagnosis of "environmental sensitivity" meant that his practical need for a window that could be opened was not officially accepted at his workplace, and that meant that he had to do his work at home and alone.

Recognizing such textually coordinated sequences of institutional action enables us to further explicate how institutional discourses organize social relations. Whereas actualities can only be known by people experientially, textual representations are accorded the authority of words that are independent of the particularities of people's experience. These are words that make it possible to generalize across the various local particularities of what was actually going on among people. They enable "textual realities" independent of those who were experiencing and acting what was actually getting done. Though what people actually do can never be exactly the same when done again or by others, people's work, as it coordinates with others, produces a standardized sequence recognizable in the terms of the relevant boss texts.

We now introduce examples of institutional ethnographic studies that explore people's work in creating textual realities that enable the practical realization of institutional courses of action. Categories or concepts of a governing/boss text establish a frame that organizes the work of constructing a textual representation that will fit it. There is then the actual work of producing what becomes the substance of the text by those responsible. Finally, once the textual representation has been established, it can then be "read" within the same frame as that which governed its making in the first place, thus enabling the ongoing of the relevant mandated course of action. The organization is much the same as that of the ideological circle, except that we are here recognizing work processes involved in the making of textually embodied accounts that then play a formal – and essential – part in the institutional course of action.

In chapter 8, we gave an account of how George Smith's research was oriented by his involvement as a gay activist. In the context of charges against the men found in a gay bathhouse, gay activists were naming issues as arising within homophobic police attitudes. Smith thought this was inadequate in terms of where to direct activist pressure on governments to make changes. We draw material and analysis from his research into the policing of the gay community as he experienced it to bring into view the making of a "textual reality." In taking up a particular experience of the policing of the gay community in Toronto, Smith reproduced a report written by police officers who visited a steambath undercover where gay men were enjoying sex. He shows how their description of what they observed was fitted to the categories of Ontario's "bawdy-house" law, thus enabling criminal charges to be brought against those found in the steambath when it was raided. We have made use below of the relevant sections in Smith's account as published (G.W. Smith, 1988) to make visible the work of producing an account of what people are doing that will fit the governing institutional categories "gay steambath." Smith cites the full text of the report produced by the police officers who went undercover into the steambath, as well as relevant passages from the Criminal Code defining a "common bawdy house." The police report contains two passages clearly designed to record activities that could be fitted to the categories of the "bawdy-house" law and hence enable those involved to be criminally prosecuted. In showing these passages here, we first cite the relevant section of the law and then show the passages from the report designed to fit the legal frame and enabling charges to be laid. Here are the relevant sections of the law enabling charges to be brought, as quoted by George Smith:

179. (1) In this Part ... 'common bawdy-house' means a place that is
      (a) kept or occupied, or
      (b) resorted to by one or more persons for the purpose of prostitution or the practice of acts of indecency ...

193. (1) Everyone who keeps a common bawdy-house is guilty of an indictable offense and is liable to imprisonment for two years.
     (2) Every one who
         (a) is an inmate of a common bawdy house,
         (b) is found, without lawful excuse, in a common bawdy-house, or
         (c) as owner, landlord, lessor, tenant, occupier, agent or otherwise having charge or control of any place, knowingly permits the place the place or any part thereof to be let or used for the purpose of a common bawdy-house, is guilty of an offence punishable on summary conviction. (G.W. Smith, 1988, p. 174)

Reproduced below is an observational passage designed to fit the frame of a section of the bawdy-house law. Those aspects of the passage that are specifically relevant are italicized:

Constables Coulis and Proctor attended at the premises, entering separately, where they approached the cash area. ... When the officers first entered the premises they walked around and noted the lay-out of the premises as well as any indecent activity that was taking place at that time. *It was at this time that both officers saw a number of men laying [sic] nude in the private booths with the door wide open. Some of these men were masturbating themselves while others just lay on the mattress watching as other men walked about the hallways.* The officers took periodic walks about the premises and they saw that the same type of indecent activity was taking place each and every time. (G.W. Smith, 1988, p. 169)

An indecent sexual act is defined by the law as an action that is done in public, that is, where it can be seen by anyone who's around. The passage from the report quoted above makes sure to show that where men were masturbating, they could be watched by others or seen casually by those walking by. These are sexual acts "in public"; they fit the frame of acts of indecency named in the law. Those found in the steambath when it was raided and arrests were made do not have to be directly involved in acts of indecency; as "inmates" of a bawdy house, a site of indecent sexuality, they can be charged.

Two other observations written into the report describe the actions of the man in charge of the steambath so as to fit the section of the bawdy-house law that specifies who can be charged in addition to those directly involved in the indecent activities: "Everyone who ... [is an] agent or otherwise having charge or control of any place or any part thereof to be let or used for the purpose of a common bawdy house, is guilty of an offence." Here are the relevant two passages (again in italics) of the report that make it clear that the "John Doe" in charge at the time of the undercover police operation was aware of what was going on and took no steps to prevent it:

> Constables Coulis and Proctor attended at the premises, entering separately, where they approached the cash area. It was at this location that the officers first saw the accused; who was later identified as [John Doe]. *Doe was the only employee that the officers saw that night. [DOE] was the one who permitted the officers access to the premises once they had paid the fee for either a room or a locker.* ...
>
> During the course of the first visit the officers made certain purchases from [DOE], who was working in the office area. The office area was equipped with numerous and sundry items available to the patrons for a fee: pop, coffee, cigarettes, Vaseline and various inhalants. *The officers watched [DOE] on two separate occasions when he left the office area to clean rooms that had just been vacated. On each of these occasions, [DOE] walked past a number of rooms that were occupied by men who were masturbating themselves. At no time did [DOE] make an effort to stop these men, or even suggest that they close the door to their booth so that these activities would no longer be visible to other club patrons.* (G.W. Smith, 1988, p. 169)

The men in the bathhouse are committing acts of indecency; the manager knew what they were doing; and the owner was accountable – they could all be charged under the "bawdy-house" laws because the undercover police described what they saw to fit the categories/wording of the (legal) boss text. The textual "reality" created by the police report had, of course, no connection with what was going on in the bathhouse setting as far as those who were involved sexually were concerned. They were just enjoying themselves.

George Smith introduces an important reminder. Though he does not explore what follows institutionally, he does locate the report in a mandated course of action organized by the frame written into the "bawdy-house" law. Following on the submission of the police report and, presumably, when the report had been reviewed (and possibly revised) by the police supervisor, it would be submitted to the city attorney, where it would be read in terms of the relevant law and charges would be issued, leading to the arrests of those found in the bathhouse, as well as the manager and the owner. At each moment in such a sequence of institutional action the circular process is put into operation, though it may not be an explicit focus of the ongoing work being done – the boss text frame organized the work of producing an account that can be read in its terms, enabling the next step in the "mandated course of action" when charges were made against those who can be identified via the report as fitting the boss text categories. And so on. It is a sequence that is initiated with the work that builds from people's actualities a representation designed to fit the "shells" of the boss text; this is how people's actualities become actionable within the institutionally mandated course of action; the textual representation establishes the continuity of "cases" with one another. In some instances, as in the police report leading to charges, the account would travel unchanged through the whole sequence, including sentencing, if that is where it ended up. In others a case file would preserve the original moment at the inception of the sequence, but would be added to as new information, records of action taken, and so on are added to the file.

The referents for the categories of institutional courses of action, though framed entirely in the relevant institutional discourse, are to be found in various forms of textual representations. Those described above fall within the general frame of law. Other forms, such as the categories of outcomes and so on that are developed with the imposition of managerial systems of accountability (Griffith and Smith, 2014), align local events and doings to an overarching managerial organization articulating an institutional economy, as we have seen in Rankin and Campbell's study of the reorganization of nurses' work within a new managerial frame. In George Smith's account, we see the building of textual representations fitting the boss text frame of law. The work of police officers going undercover into the gay bathhouse and then the work of writing up a report fitted to the terms of the law shows how producing the textual representation fitting the frame of the law made the actualities of the gay experience in the steambath into a criminal act chargeable under that very law. Once a report such as that created by the police officers has become established as the ground for institutional action, it becomes the textual reality upon which the legally mandated course of action will be based and will be drawn on at different stages. To all intents and purposes, it has become reality. The action that is taken is done by and happens to real people in real time. The "found-ins" at the steambath, and its manager and its owner, are arrested and "charged." The work of inscribing actualities to fit the shell of an institutional category of the governing or boss text is what makes actualities actionable within the institutional frame.

To this point, we have emphasized how people's work produces textual representations of what has been or is going on that will fit authorized institutional frames integral to sequences of institutional action. In a recent paper, Dorothy writes (2016) about how to recognize words as practices so that we can incorporate them into our ethnographies. She gives a number of examples of frames that are nominals referring to some actual object or situation, thereby showing the difference between the standardized recognition of objects that Luria (1961, 1976) drew our attention to and the institutional frames that call on people to organize out of actuality what can be represented as fitting the institutional frame. One example Dorothy gives introduces an additional dimension, namely textual representations in which people are actively involved in producing actualities to fit the frame. She draws on J.W. Gibson's study (1986) of the war in Vietnam, which Gibson calls a "technowar." During the Vietnam War, the United States introduced statistical modes of evaluating the relative numbers of U.S. forces and the combined forces of the North Vietnamese Army (NVA) and the Vietcong (VC) as a way of evaluating effectiveness. The long-term objective of winning the war was defined as the reduction of the NVA and VC to the point where they were no longer able to replace casualties and eventually would give up – hence the creation of the "body count" as an on-the-ground objective contributing directly to the statistical data evaluating the progress of the war. Producing the body count was a developed organizational performance. It could be incorporated into evaluating the performance of military leaders in addition to individual military units. And when it came to counting the dead on the other side, it was not always clear who was an enemy and who was just a civilian Vietnamese non-combatant. Sometimes the actualities to be fitted to the shell of the "body count" had to be "performed" as, for example, when attacks were launched to provoke a response, thus enabling the killing of "enemy" Vietnamese, who could be included in a body count.

Institutional Circuits

Stimulated by Rankin and Campbell's study *Managing to Nurse* (2006), Alison and Dorothy had become aware of research that in various institutional settings focused on aspects of how new managerial controls were reorganizing front-line work. We wanted both to get discussion going around the issues that people were uncovering in various institutional settings and to move beyond particular studies to see if we could begin to describe what was going on at a more general level in Canadian governance. In a workshop, we brought together institutional ethnographers who were researching in this general topic area. We wanted presentations of their works in progress and for us to begin to develop a broader picture of new managerial regimes so that we could learn from each other how public-sector governance was being reshaped. Over a two-year period, the researchers worked on the papers they had read and discussed at the workshop, and then we had a book collection on new public management to edit (Griffith and Smith, 2014).

The notion of an institutional circuit emerged as we drew out the thread that connected the various studies. The concept of institutional circuits draws attention to how workers at the "front line" of public service organizations were responsive to the particularities of the people they were working with, while at the same time being accountable to managerially standardizing frames. This was the thread that we could use to enable the varied studies to connect in disclosing the different aspects of public governance in the public sectors. The concept "institutional circuits" suggests directions for ethnographic exploration into ruling relations organizing front-line work. It does not prescribe, but rather opens up possibilities for discovering how people's work is organized managerially, suggesting connections beyond what is locally observable and can be discovered from people's local work experience.

In the early days of institutional ethnography, we established a seminar at the Ontario Institute for Studies in Education for institutional ethnographers who had completed their doctoral degrees and graduate students still at work on theirs. We were astonished and impressed by how institutional researches in very different institutional settings could speak to one another. We could learn and see more and more as we began to be able to recognize or look for analogous forms of organizing in very different settings. The concept of institutional circuits that provided a thread linking the different studies in our book on new public management (Griffith and Smith, 2014) aimed at drawing attention to the studies, which were very different in the concreteness of their actual situations, yet which could be seen to bring into view major changes going on in our societies and, as Marie Campbell (2014) emphasizes, the changes establishing the textual foundations of global governance.

The first contribution to the substantive part of our book is Richard Darville's study (2014) of how adult literacy programs designed collaboratively by the educator and the learner, with objectives worked out between them, became subject to standardization with predetermined objectives for the learner. The management frame was reset to make the outcomes of adult literacy programs across Canada commensurable. The changes oriented literacy training not towards the actual situation and interests of learners, but towards the standardized and internationally comparable skills of a labour force. In the second chapter, Marie Campbell (2014) describes the reorganizing of an international non-governmental organization (INGO) working in Kyrgyzstan with the implementing of the 2005 Paris Declaration on Aid Effectiveness and its recommended management by results (MBR) strategy. Campbell has a special interest in the texts establishing the new managerial organization and how they coordinate the work of those active in the INGO. Within the new regime, "effectiveness is accomplished textually" (Campbell, 2014, p. 73). Campbell's ethnography of project development by the INGO in Kyrgyzstan is "an entry point to how MBR ... works in practice" (Campbell, 2014, p. 60). She brings into focus just how the preparation of a project proposal requires using the new management language in translating and modifying objectives to fit the authorized categories: "The project participants ... are developing the individual capacity to calculate and represent their activities-in-texts as part of a global knowledge regime constituting the information environment for managing and funding 'effectively'" (Campbell, 2014, p. 61). The studies by Darville and by Campbell are very different, with different subjects, but both make observable the relations between the textually organized managerial organization and how it works out in what actual people are doing. Neither study used nor needed the concept of institutional circuit; that was our term for the thread we discovered as we assembled the diverse papers as chapters of our edited book.

But one group actually made use of the concept in their analysis. Marjorie Devault, Murali Venkatesh, and Frank Ridzi (2014) adapted the notion of institutional circuits as "accountability circuits" to explore the work organization put in place in a county in New York state as the county administration of the chronic care aspect of the federal Medicaid regulations was running into a problem with its application process. Applications for support for those in chronic care could only be made when patients could document that their own resources had run out. The required process is complex and detailed, and there is a 90-day limit after support has been lost. It might take a senior a long time to gather the required information, and if the time limit was passed, the chronic care homes where some of those making applications were resident could end up providing care without receiving payment from the state. Social work staff in the care facilities would work with seniors to meet the eligibility requirements, but there were still problems.

Accountability circuits are usually hierarchical, but these authors show us what they call a "lateral" accountability circuit. New management in the Medicaid unit in the county sought a way to work out the problems the various county facilities caring for seniors were experiencing by establishing a collaborative arrangement: the social work staff of the facilities would become responsible for delivering the eligibility applications; they would get specialized training; and appropriate textual forms were devised for trained facility staff to complete. The authors describe the textual organization of that work as follows:

> Given the thoroughly text-mediated character of Medicaid's complex provisions, it is not surprising that change required yet more texts. ... The fact that innovation occurs in such textual forms provides evidence of the ways that texts coordinate front-line action. The Unit's ensemble of support texts intended for caseworkers can be sorted into four categories: lists, task aids, information sheets, and templates. The checklist, for example, specifies the kinds of evidentiary documentation required for a complete and valid application. Tasks aids offer instructions for completing a task or a step in a task such as the 'Income Tax Returns' form. ... A third category of support text provides supplemental information on completing the Medicaid application, such as the sheet on 'Information Notice to Couples with Institutionalized Spouses.' Templates are the most coercive in intent and are designed to restrict user input to checking boxes, circling options, and filling in blanks, often requiring a stark 'yes' or 'no' response when there may well be a complex story to tell. (DeVault et al. 2014, p. 190)

This was the reorganization DeVault, Venkatesh, and Ridzi explored. They conclude that in their efforts to reform the procedure, the "reformers" work with two "accountability circuits":

> On the one hand, they are accountable to the 'boss text' of the program legislation; they must work within the parameters of enabling regulations. At the same time, they have responded to a different set of local accountabilities, working with those in other organizations (the hospitals and long-term care facilities in the county) also charged with the provision of care for the elderly. By responding not only to their legal mandate, but also to the concerns of the facilities that depend on Medicaid reimbursement, these reformers have forged and strengthened a local and horizontal accountability circuit that links organizational entities in the county in unprecedented new ways. They have enlisted trained facility workers to assist overburdened eligibility staff at the Unit in a new division of labour; they have also reorganized Medicaid intake work to align it with the business interests of the facilities. In return for this responsiveness to facilities the Unit asked those organizations to be accountable to it by co-operating in the new division of labour. (DeVault et al., 2014, p. 194)

The notion of circuit points to an exploration of how people at work are realizing – making real – the textual imaginary vested in institutional boss texts as actual sequences of action, accountable to those very texts.

Although we, Alison and Dorothy, had designed the notion of institutional circuits to explicate common threads in the papers in our collection and not to guide research, Devault, Venkatesh, and Ridzi's work shows that it has possibilities for explicating the managerial organization of public service work. Their concept of "accountability circuits" is a very useful specification, particularly useful in the context of the changes in public-sector management that have been taking place. Let's be clear, however, that the concept of institutional circuits was developed to explicate a thread connecting more generally the various studies that came together in our 2009 workshop on how people's work was being reorganized with the introduction of new forms of management into public services. This interest originated in Rankin and Campbell's study, *Managing to Nurse* (2006), and since that study, other institutional ethnographies have taken up this issue in exploring how the local work experiences of front-line workers is reorganized as new forms of management are imposed. An example is Nicola Waters's (2015) study of the problems of nurses who specialize in wound care as various new forms of standardizing their practices are imposed. Waters does not use this concept; we do not expect that; rather, we emphasize its practical uses, in directing research attention to aspects of how ruling relations are organized as actual practices that may otherwise go unobserved.

In Conclusion

This chapter has brought into view some of the ways institutional ethnographers have discovered and explicated how ruling relations enter into people's everyday practices and, as conceptualized in this chapter, have potential uses in making observable some of the distinctive forms of coordinating the institutional and the local. The three concepts we have laid out here – ideological circles, textual realities, and institutional circuits – open up rather than confine research directions. We have shown in our three examples how powerfully the concepts of ideological circles, textual realities, and institutional circuits can be when they are brought into play in developing ethnographies. We can also see that rather than confining and imposing final interpretations, they open up possible further lines of research as they tie what is brought into focus into further relational connections.

At this point we need a reminder of the technological capacity of replicable texts that in a sense stabilizes the essential historicity of human life. The various circles or circuits that institutional ethnographers have been bringing into view create an almost magical world of representation in which what has actually been going on can be categorized using the institutionally authorized categories and concepts and entered into ongoing courses of institutionally organized action. The institutional categories, as applied by people in their work, enable representations of actualities which displace those actualities as people know and experience them. Deveau's account of being trapped in the ideological circle that displaced the local actualities of his disability is a powerful instance of how this sequence works. Deveau's experience was painful and makes especially visible the disappearance of his actual experiences in the process he analyses in its working as an ideological circle. His observations are exemplary in that he explicates his own experience of having to enter into and practise the very ideological circle that traps him.

Research that engages sequences of institutional action should be aware of how the textual representations and the governing concepts and categories that organize them translate what is actually going on and getting done among people into the institutional language of the authorized and authorizing texts. If Dorothy and Alison could have explored ethnographically Alison's experience of what she described to herself as "institution talk," we would likely have been discovering a similar organization of standardized categories displacing, in people's "work talk," what they are actually talking about. Teachers working in Ontario will know just how to locate aspects of their classroom organization as "levels," catching whatever they are talking about (or just thinking about) in the real world into the institutional discourse of Ontario's Education Quality and Accountability Office. We recognize here how the ongoing historicity of people's actual doings and the textual realities get articulated to the textually replicated frames of the institutionally authorized texts.

Chapter Ten

Making Change from Below

At the very beginnings of institutional ethnography and long before it had a name, Dorothy was active in developing research that would serve projects for change emerging, at that time, in the women's movement in British Columbia. In our first and introductory chapter, we described as an important moment Dorothy's initiatives in creating a women's research centre in Vancouver, where she worked with graduate students from the Anthropology/Sociology Department of the University of British Columbia. Dorothy also became involved with the organizational leadership of Gene Errington and the support of the province's New Democratic Party (NDP) of that time, with initiatives emerging in the isolated and single-industry towns of the BC interior. Some of the work she did with women in such isolated towns taught her to learn from women's actual situations what were concretely the issues and problems of their everyday lives that the possibility of making change brought into view. Rather than the standardizing of issues in feminist terms, it became important to locate specifically what were the practical difficulties the women in these communities were experiencing. For example, Dorothy remembers in one hilly community how the issue for women living up the hill was the walls of snow built up by snow ploughs on streets with no sidewalks, which made getting downtown to do the shopping with a child in a pram very dangerous. The women wanted sidewalks. That was their issue and that was the issue we worked with.

Institutional ethnography's beginnings were thus linked closely to the pragmatics of making change from below. In chapter 8 we described how institutional ethnographers have developed explorations of ruling that are grounded in issues and problems that have arisen in the researchers' own lives. They offer ethnographies that make the dimensions of the problems fully explicit. Chapter 9 presented George

Smith's investigation of how the undercover police officers' report of what was going on in a gay bathhouse was written to fit what the men could be seen as doing into chargeable offences under Ontario's "bawdy-house" law. Specific changes were not proposed. Rather, Smith's analysis was clearly intended to inform activists of what they were actually confronting in efforts to make change and what kinds of objectives would be effective. There is, however, also research that is very focused on making specific changes.

In this chapter, we turn to research directly linked to making change. There are, indeed, so many ways that institutional ethnography can be brought into play in opening up the actualities of how people's work is organized, work that can come to be seen as relevant to change and could be the topic of a whole book. Here, however, we describe two projects that used institutional ethnography to open up just how ruling relations create problems and identifying just where changes should be and can be made. Both are concerned, though very differently, with issues for women of "domestic abuse" or "sexual violence." Ellen Pence became involved in IE early on. She came from Duluth, Minnesota, to work with Dorothy, and eventually completed her doctoral dissertation, *Safety for Battered Women in a Textually Mediated Legal System*, in 1996. The major focus of her work became promoting consciousness of the need for change and the practicalities of making it in the community and, more specifically, among those occupational groups – police, city lawyers and office staff, social workers, probation officers, and so on – at work in the judicial processing of "domestic abuse."

Our second focus is on the work of Susan Turner, Julia Bomberry, and Amye Werner, who prepared a report on how sexual-violence complaints were being handled by police on the Six Nations Reserve in Ontario. Their research was funded by the Ontario Ministry of Community Security and Correctional Services, and on the basis of their research they were able to make specific recommendations for change, many of which have been taken up by the ministry.

Ellen Pence and Making Institutional Change

Ellen Pence was active in the 1980 founding of the Domestic Abuse Intervention Project (DAIP) in Duluth, Minnesota. DAIP worked with the police, set up a program of education for wife-batterers, and conducted training sessions for police and other professionals involved internationally. As laws prohibiting wife-beating came to be widely enacted in the United States, implementation was imperfect. DAIP became aware of the developing problems of those who were victims of abuse but whose issues of safety, security, and welfare were institutionally bypassed. Pence's dissertation, with Dorothy as supervisor, focused on the civil and criminal court processing of domestic abuse, using interviews with practitioners, such as police responding to domestic abuse calls, lawyers, social workers, probation officers, and so on.

The first time Dorothy visited Ellen Pence in Duluth, she went to a meeting organized by Ellen that brought together police, the city attorney, and social workers and other practitioners in the local judicial process. The meeting was informal, but its focus was on what those present could see as possible ways of improving the institutionalized practices of the judicial processing of "cases" of domestic abuse. As Ellen's work brought together her practical experience of working with DAIP and what she had learned from institutional ethnography in her work for her dissertation, she developed an analysis of how the various institutional practitioners were involved in the judicial sequence of action, beginning with the 911 call, the police patrol investigation, and the police report – the primary text organizing the judicial sequence.

At each step in the process, the institutional language and requirements of the practitioners came into play in organizing the "case" as the textually embodied focus, and in how it was taken up and moved forward. In a sense, the different institutional practitioners set up a case to be worked with using their specialized institutional discourse and rules of practice. While those who connected directly with the victim or victims of a given happening might be aware of the dimension of the issues and problems victims were experiencing, the institutional discourse and practice excluded opening up possibilities for remedial action.

Pence's thinking was developing in her ongoing dialogue with institutional ethnography as well as with her experiences of working with the various institutional practitioners involved in the judicial processing of domestic abuse. The judicial process had no way of taking into account or even recognizing what victims of abuse might have experienced or be experiencing over its course. Pence talked to and brought practitioners into collective conversations, and explored with them ways in which they might become more responsive to issues for victims. She had set up an organization, now Praxis International, which applied and further developed these approaches to transforming the professional practices of the judicial process. An early device was the Praxis Institutional Audit:

Audits may not keep people from embezzling but they do tend to draw everyone's attention to proper financial documentation at least once a year. I am using the concept of an audit in order to evoke that same image and that sense of examining practices. However, I am proposing that unlike a financial audit conducted by an outsider, an institutional audit be conducted by a team both of advocates and of practitioners within the legal system. A safety audit can be both an investigative and an organizing tool. As an investigative process it will dispel the myth of the objective investigation of crimes and explicate how the ideological processes of ruling are at work in these cases. As an organizing process it can be designed to involve an interdisciplinary team which includes community-based advocates in an effort to facilitate the process of proposing and implementing changes in legal system. (Pence, 2001, p. 226)

Pence and Melanie Shepard designed a workbook distributed by Praxis that communities could make use of in initiating auditing projects among local institutional practitioners (see Shepard and Pence, 1999). Their work was supported by the United States Justice Foundation, which gave considerable financial assistance and also supported the distribution of Praxis innovations throughout the United States.

An example of one of the significant changes introduced was in the police procedures for investigating the situation of reported abuse. In one chapter of her dissertation, Ellen contrasts the marked differences in the sentencing outcomes of two cases. In one case, the person found guilty was a man of some standing in the community, a professional with no criminal record; the other was a member of a local Indigenous group who had a record of being charged with being drunk in charge of a car and other offences. The former got a sentence of probation and community service, no jail time; the latter a jail sentence. But DAIP knew more. The first man had a history of violent controlling behaviour over his wife. The second man's episode of hitting his wife happened when they were both drunk; it had happened once before on a similar occasion, but there was nothing compared with the background story of the first man's abuse. How was it that the history of the first abuser would be invisible to the police, or, if indeed they became aware, was not entered into the police report that constituted the case and reproduced throughout what Ellen calls the "processing interchanges" of the judicial process? The police report in the final version is not only the basis on which charges can be laid but is also an integral part of the sentencing review documentation. Police initiatives emerging from Pence's discussions with them introduced significant changes in how police responded to a "domestic" call. The police arriving at the site would interview those involved separately and learn not only of the immediate event but what had been going on in the partners' lives, thus ensuring that the victim's experience could be adequately incorporated into the police report. Though the charges might not be changed, the sentencing could take into account the information about what had been going in the domestic partners' lives, such as a history of domestic violence and control, which would now be contained in the report.

As mentioned, Pence became founding director of an organization, Praxis International: "The primary goal of Praxis was to develop a method and process of examining institutional practices and their impact on women's lives." And "Praxis means action, but not just any kind of action. It is the application of a science or an art to practical work—in other words, action that results from thinking things through" (Praxis International, 2020). Pence used her institutional ethnographic connection not only as a way for her to open up how to discover and explicate the judicial processing of domestic abuse cases in ways that take into account the situation of the victim whose life is deeply affected in institutionally invisible ways; she also went further by developing a new theoretical framework, called "institutional analysis" (Pence and Smith, 2011). Based on institutional ethnography, it provides a generalized guide for involving institutional practitioners as well as advocates for change in a critical reviewing of the hidden implications for victims of abuse of institutional practices. And it establishes a method for practitioners to become aware of problems created for women by their institutional practices and for exploring with other practitioners what and how changes could be made.

The Six Nations Report: Building Change On and Off Reserve

Early in 2015, the Ontario Ministry of Community Safety and Correctional Services (MCSCS) sought applicants for a project to explore "Police responses to sexual violence and harassment of aboriginal women and girls." Susan Turner had been working for the previous few years with the Ganohkwasra Family Assault Support Services Centre on the Six Nations Reserve on a project exploring services for women who experienced sexual violence. The director, Sandra Montour, asked Turner to make a formal application for the funded project with them as partners working with their police; it was accepted. Since Turner was already working with the organization, she could connect the formally funded project with manager Julia Bomberry and researcher Amye Werner, both of whom worked in the Family Assault Centre on the reserve. Working together, they undertook a study titled "Police Responses to Sexual Violence and Harassment Against Aboriginal Women and Girls 2015–2016 Program of the Six Nations Reserve." The research for the report submitted to the ministry relied on their institutional ethnography research as the foundation for its recommendations – which have been taken up by the ministry in making change. Their ethnography was also presented at an IE workshop arranged by Liza McCoy for the International Sociology Association (ISA) meetings in the summer of 2018.

The people of the Six Nations Reserve continue their traditional cultures as their way of life, including their language. The research undertaken by Susan, Julia, and Amye is an ethnography of the social organization of the policing of "sexual violence" on the reserve; it describes just how the policing of complaints categorized as "violence, domestic violence, and sexual assault" engages the work of the police and how what they get done on the reserve hooks up with the regional services such as the hospital, sexual assault centre, victim services, and court system outside of the reserve. The police are themselves members of the Reserve Nations; their policing practices are those defined and mandated within the complex of relations of the Ontario system of law and policing. Their local work is organized institutionally under Ontario regulations. At the same time, their actual practices get done in the context of the culture of the local First Nations community.

Turner conducted extended and in-depth interviews at all levels – perhaps better described as conversations –with the reserve police. Turner's mapping procedures were used to bring into view the actual sequences of work and text, including how governing texts, such as the standardized sequences of policing action, were built into the Ontario legal system. The mapping was a procedure that, apart from its significance in writing the ethnographic aspects of the report, was also of value to police and off-reserve services front-line participants in bringing to their awareness just how their own work practices entered into and were organized as part of extended institutional sequences.

The secondary dialogic moving from the research engagement with people to the ethnography brings very vividly forward how the institutional categories and concepts of the governmental texts organize the work of the police. The ethnography shows just how the mandated sequences of policing and court action get done as actual work processes, including the everyday constraints of time and the availability of those with specialized experience to undertake the recording of the "complaint," using the institutionally required categories and procedures.

Six Nations police officers may be aware of the multiple layers and complexities of sexual violence on reserve, but must work with and follow the Criminal Code guidelines, language, procedures, and categories in information gathering at the scene and determining severity of violence. (Turner et al., 2017, p. 27)

The ability of police to respond to the victim's situation as they experience what she may be going through and their relation as community members to her situation is bound by the practicalities of time available. "[G]iven there is no Sexual Assault Unit – SNPS [Six Nations Police Services] must also take into consideration how time consuming the investigation will be" (Turner et al., 2017, pp. 17–18). The ethnography makes visible officers' actual working conditions, including being underfunded and understaffed or resourced and without any sexual-violence officers. The ethnography also featured the community orientation of the officers. The police policy analyst commented:

> I believe the officers do some community-based practices and they're very cognizant of that, but it doesn't always translate into "good policy," for lack of a better word. ... The amount of time sometimes that they spend speaking with a victim, or doing the smaller things that our people will respond to, are not reflected in any of the policy or procedures that we have. It's 'interview the victim –"period."' It doesn't go into the nuances of stuff that they do when they're actually in the interview, to make the victim feel safe, secure, calm, protected, in order for them to share what happened to them. It is very difficult to get that onto paper because they do it in practice ... they deal with something and it's on to the next thing. (Turner et al., 2017, p. 14)

The ethnography brings into view problems that are integral to police practices that could not be solved under the conditions existing at the time of the research and the report. In the report conclusion and in the authors' later presentation, the Government of Ontario and its ministries are called upon to give priority to six "Actions":

1 Equitably fund SNPS [Six Nations Police Services].
2 Support the addition of a SNPS sexual assault unit or special officers.
3 Establish, fund and support a SNPS Victim Services on Six Nations.
4 Establish and provide secure funding to a SN [Six Nations] Sexual Assault Centre and recognize SN sexual assault counsellors.
5 Work with ministry partners to fund and provide secure funding for more SNPS officers, training, initiatives, related to human trafficking, MMIW [Missing and Murdered Indigenous Women] and youth.
6 Support the Six Nations Police high risk initiatives; Community-Minded Practices Protocol and the development of a SNPS Safety Assessment Tool. (Turner et al., 2017, p. 67)

Though we cannot yet provide in detail the action taken by the Ministry of Community Safety and Correctional Services, the ministry has responded to the "Actions" called for and sustained as issues by the ethnographic account of police responses to complaints of sexual violence, by making at least some of the changes called for, including providing equitable salaries for the SNPS officers, who had been paid at lower rates than police outside reserves, and funding a Six Nations Sexual Assault Centre, Six Nations Victim Services, and Ganohkwasra's sexual assault prevention training for front-line workers.

Conclusion

These two institutional ethnographically grounded projects for change aim to address specific problems of how institutional practices are done in definite local settings of people's work. Though both are concerned with issues of violence against women, they are very different both in directions of exploration and in how they approached actually bringing about change. Pence focused on the judicial process from the standpoint of the women who were victims of the abuse but who disappear as the judicial process moves forward except as they may participate as witnesses in court proceedings. Pence does not aim at just discovering what is happening to victims; rather, she aims at the institutional practitioners whose distinctive professional discourse and work requirements displace the ongoing and everyday of victims' lives. Her objective is to make visible to practitioners how victims' lives become effectively invisible and to propose ways in which they can begin to examine and take on the making of changes in institutional practices so as to make those lives visible and open up possibilities for remedial action. The aim is not for one particular jurisdiction, but to provide methods that those in such situations who become aware of the problems of victims' invisibility can use in beginning to reform their own institutional practices. The institutional analysis Pence developed aims at generalizing critical practices for practitioners at the different parts of judicial procedures in cases of domestic abuse. One outcome of her approach to change was a radical transformation of police responses to "domestic abuse" calls. Formerly, there had been the recurrent problem that, when it came to charges and, eventually, if someone was found guilty, the penalties applied, no account had been taken of the history of control and abuse except for what was recorded in the legal archives. In association with Duluth police, Pence designed a new approach that eventually became the standard for police forces in the United States (should they be concerned with these issues and wish to make such changes).

By contrast, the IE approach applied by Turner, Bomberry, and Werner in the Six Nations Reserve focused very specifically on just how the local police operate in relation to complaints of sexual violence under the legal and police services procedures standardized across the Province of Ontario. The authors' ethnographic research made visible how the police work was getting done in actual situations and how it hooked up to the services and court procedures beyond the reserve. The ethnographic account of the day-to-day working conditions and institutionalized practices in the local settings of First Nations Peoples living with and within their traditional culture makes visible the specifics of how the work gets done and where the problems are. On this basis, very specific recommendations could be made, and they were followed up by the ministry concerned and other ministries the report called on.

Both of these projects engage with issues of passionate concern, but are very differently situated. Ellen's focus is always on the work organization of those professionals whose work is integral to the judicial processing of the legal category of "domestic abuse" and its invisible consequences for the women involved. Susan, Julia, and Amy focus on how the police do their work on the Six Nations Reserve in response to a complaint of sexual violence, aiming at securing changes from the relevant Ontario ministry that will improve how provincial legislation is applied in the Indigenous setting of the Six Nations Reserve. Though clearly the second of the two was very effective in securing changes, Ellen goes beyond specific change. Her aim and achievement was to create a method of analysis drawing on IE that professionals could draw into the process of analysing their own work practices, including the use of language, for ways of changing the institutional practices that their analysis – using Ellen's method – brings to light. But there is also a hidden gain from the Six Nations Reserve study. Susan's mapping methods (www.mappingforchange.ca) were used to explore with the police how they did the work of taking up a complaint of sexual harassment. In this process, police became aware of how their work was actually getting done and how to see problems and possibilities for change they had not considered before.

The two introduce for us a potential for institutional ethnography that is not perhaps fully recognized as having a distinctive significance for the research we do. As we've shown in earlier chapters, problems people actually experience are of major importance for research directions. But a move towards discoveries of how changes can be made is a bold step forward and needs to be more adequately recognized for its value to our field.

PART FOUR

Conclusion

Chapter Eleven

In Conclusion

In this inconclusive concluding chapter, we want to make clear that we have not attempted an overall assessment of institutional ethnography; we are simply working through and organizing what we have learned in our many years of conversation with the work of institutional ethnographers and also with each other in the course of writing this book. In this chapter, we are also looking for what is emerging for us out of that experience as possible directions for further inquiry. Institutional ethnography always takes up what actual people are doing and experiencing. As we described in chapter 2, learning from people's experience is an important moment for many institutional ethnographers, including learning from their own experience, as Alison and Dorothy did when we started to explore how mothers' work in the home related to the work of schools (Griffith and Smith, 2005). In chapter 1, we introduced a passage from Marx and Engels's *The German Ideology* in which they ask the question that has become ours: "Individuals always started and start from themselves. Their relations are the relations of their real life. How does it happen that their relations assume an independent existence over against them?" (Marx and Engels, 1976, p. 14). They, of course, are posing this question of relations organized by money; Marx did some extensive thinking about how monetary interchange introduces a mediating abstraction that displaces the particularity of person-to-person relating. This is the grounding of economic relations, and these, of course, are the focus of Marx and Engels's thinking and research. Institutional ethnography, however, focuses on governing relations grounded in replicated written texts (whether print or electronic or ...); their textual grounding enables them to have an independent existence over against us, and they overpower our lives, as do those relations mediated by money. What we in IE are exploring as we take up people's experiences is how we are engaged in and with the textually objectified forms of governance that have become fundamental to discovering aspects of that work we had not seen when we started, and which, we can begin now to see, reaches beyond it. Developing a topic here suggested the next thread or evoked a discovery of such a thread that we had not seen when we started. In this concluding chapter, we want to make clear that, although we've drawn extensively on the work of institutional ethnography, we cannot claim a generalized knowledge of the field and have no overall assessment to offer as a conclusion. And yet we have arrived somewhere. Hence, in this last chapter, we have not called it a "conclusion." Rather, we will take a look at what might come next in building upon the institutional ethnographic work that has engaged our conversation. Where should we, Alison and Dorothy, take institutional ethnography beyond where we have arrived? We are looking now for what can be explored further, drawing on the work that we have brought together in the preceding chapters.

If institutional ethnographic research is always to be grounded in actual people, their doings and experiences, we have to be committed to learning *from* them about their experience and know-how. In exploring this approach in the early chapters of this book, we sought to find out more of what was involved in drawing on people's experience, including our own. "Experience" is not simply what actually happened or was getting done; it is always a selective practice of a moment of self-dialogue. We could see then that as researchers learn from people's experiential knowledge, there is a dialogue, in which the researcher's interests are engaged. But if the work of collecting data as we learned from people we talked to or watched had an essentially dialogic organization, the process of then writing an ethnography was a second dialogue in which the researcher works with what s/he has learned to create an ethnographic account – built from what has been learned, but now bringing into view interconnections that would go beyond any particular observations or experience. In Part II of this book, we introduced three concepts that we have come to see as useful in organizing the researcher's dialogue with the actual people whose lives and work the researcher is learning about. We were clear that these three concepts – discourse, work (in the generous sense), and texts – were not *theoretical* in the sense of imposing interpretations or explanations on data; they were what have proven to be useful *guides* to focus the ethnographers' interest in asking questions, in wanting to know more, or in what to attend to and record when making observations. Yes, the ethnographer is listening and encouraging the respondent to go ahead and tell just how it is for them, but the ethnographer needs to know more about what has been described or needs to open up topics that matter to him or her but which may not have been mentioned by the respondent. These three concepts can be useful to researchers in reminding them what information they may need to build the ethnography.

The next stage, the work of actually creating an ethnography, is a second dialogue in which the researcher engages with what has been learned from respondents and/or from her or his own observations, aiming at an ethnography for readers participating in IE discourse. It may involve returning to original or new sources, since developing the ethnography may bring into view gaps or unexpected findings that need more exploring. There is, indeed, the ordinary problem that an institutional ethnography has no automatic boundaries, since such boundaries do not exist in the world that is being explored. The research process could be thought of as being built as it goes along. In introducing some of the research we have learned from, we thought it useful to describe examples of how research is given direction by its starting place in the specific concerns and interests of the researcher. We learned from the work of George Smith, Gerald de Montigny, and Janet Rankin and Marie Campbell how issues and problems arising in their own lives led them to a "problematic" that organized the direction of their research. We can see very clearly in each of these research approaches how the researchers' interests and concerns organize what is opened up for investigation and what discoveries are made. This, of course, is antithetical to standard sociological practice which is committed to at least the appearance of objectivity; research direction and focus is specified theoretically, perhaps even with definite hypotheses to be tested, but at least using a language that dissociates the sociological account from the particularities of the sociologist's interests or those of the people whose practices in the everyday world become the research objects. Institutional ethnography, as we have suggested earlier, relies for its commitment to telling the truth by working out accounts that rely on what people are and have been actually doing – and so discovering, at the ethnography writing stage, just how what they do is coordinated into sequences of action (G.W. Smith, 1995). Starting from interests and concerns in which the researcher participates directs investigation into the complexes of relations that do not automatically sort themselves neatly into relevant and irrelevant ones.

Chapter 9 brings into view something of what has been made observable by researchers working with institutional ethnography. In people's practices, textual representations built from but displacing what is actually going on or is being done become the grounding of institutional courses of action. Deveau describes how the governing categories of disabilities policies displace the actualities he experiences as a disabled person. His account is especially vivid because he is writing from and of his experience of his ideological subsumption as he engages with a governing authority to get the workplace environment he needs. George Smith describes how the report of undercover cops observing gay sexual behaviour in a bathhouse is designed to fit Ontario's "bawdy-house" law, enabling charges to be brought against those "found in." DeVault, Venkatesh, and Ridzi bring into view the managerial organization of accountability circuits in their account of the work of establishing senior eligibility for chronic care support. What can be seen in retrospect is how these new forms of management in public institutions, a major focus of Rankin and Campbell's *Managing to Nurse* (chapter 8), are creating modes of subjecting the front-line work of public service workers to performance and/or outcome requirements designed to fit managerial evaluations of efficiency adapted from the managerial systems of corporate capital. Work oriented to individuals in providing public services cannot be organized the same way as methods of mass production. Here is how Wikipedia describes mass production:

> Mass production involves making many copies of products, very quickly, using assembly line techniques to send partially complete products to workers who each work on an individual step, rather than having a worker work on a whole product from start to finish. (Wikipedia, 2020)

Public services, however, engage with actual individuals, who cannot be processed the way products are in mass production. Standardizing practices are used to override human individuality in services such as health care or education that work with actual people – for example, the standardized tests that generate "levels" of students in the classroom for Ontario teachers. Work oriented to individuals in the provision of public services cannot be organized as in methods of mass production whereby standardized parts can be produced separately and eventually assembled. Public services engage with actual people as they are. Each is unique and uniquely situated. Technologies have been and are being developed that displace people's unique situations and experiences and select what fits the standardizing frames of management, restricting service responses by front-line staff to standardized performances or outcomes that are tied into the monetary values of contemporary managerial systems. Liza McCoy's (1999) research on Ontario's college system brings into view how managerial modes of organizing and control adapted from corporate management practices are applied in the public sector. Her study focuses on the installation of accounting practices aimed at increasing "efficiency" – improving the "quality" of service and reducing costs. These are "documentary practices that discover and represent in calculable and comparable terms relevant administrative objects such as measurable inputs and outputs, unit costs, transaction volumes, rates of error or wastage, length of time for service delivery, customer satisfaction, efficiency, etc." (McCoy, 1999, p. 9). These managerial accounting practices are used to translate organizational activities into numbers that can be accorded monetary value and that also enable comparisons to be made across different agencies.

We have been learning how what has been going on with people becomes caught up in an ordering of what they do that they have not chosen. The notion of "institutional circuits" directs attention to what people are doing, going from what's actually going on to a standardized representation conforming to the language and framing of the boss text (chapters 8 and 9). This displacing of what is actually going on in people's lives when they are caught up in the textual representations of institutional order is a thread linking the work we have drawn together here. Institutional courses of action depend, as they are activated, on textual representations. Gay men's sexual enjoyment in the police-raided bathhouse is irrelevant to the charges brought against them for sexual indecency under Ontario's "bawdy-house" law (see chapter 9); a nurse's own awareness of a patient's problems has to be set aside as she conforms to the requirements of the electronic system of hospital bed allocation (chapter 8); the historical continuities of the people of the Six Nations Reserve have no place (at least for now) in how the Six Nations police, themselves members of that culture, take up and report sexual violence within the Ontario legal system (chapter 10).

The text-mediated governing or ruling relations take on an independent existence over against us and overpower our lives. As we emphasized, Marx and Engels looked towards relations mediated by money and here we have been opening up for exploration those relations that are mediated by texts and especially by those written in institutional languages. It is hard to remember now, but in the early days of the women's movement, women had to struggle with the absence of words in which to speak our everyday experiences of masculine oppression. Let us be clear here: this was how our relations with men were organized; it was not simply women's personal choices. It was how our relations were organized socially by relations "over against us." Though we had the right to vote, we had no voice in the public sphere, in academe, in poetry, in music, in the media, or in governing. Though we could for sure exchange recipes and child care and household tips, we could not talk with each other about our experiences with men. And in many settings, such as education or politics, women were not the authorities, not those to be listened to. Dorothy remembers how before the women's movement, when she was concluding a lecture and looking for questions, she always looked towards the men in the classroom, never at the women. We began to make changes; we began to listen to one another seriously; we found words to express the actualities of our lives to one another. Experiences such as the violence of male partners in the home, which had been unspoken among us, began to find expression as there began to be books, talks, little newspapers, that gave expression to women. We learned words to speak our experiences and women who would listen and who we would listen to.

Gillian Walker's *Family Violence and the Women's Movement: The Conceptual Politics of Struggle* (1990) is an ethnography of the conceptual politics of women's movement struggles to enter women's issues into government practices and policies. The Battered Women's Movement, focusing on women's experience of domestic violence in Canada, aimed to secure government response to problems in the everyday of women's lives. It brought together communities of struggle among different organizations expressing different experiences by developing concepts that could be shared among them without displacing the particularities of women's experiences of violence. Concepts were needed to express women's experience of violence, but they were also to be concepts that would fit with relevant government functions. As government departments took up the issues being raised, the concepts originally designed to express women's experience were reorganized and re-framed in the new objectified mode that engaged them in the institutional circuits – see chapter 10 – selectively fitting women's actual experiences of being battered into the textual representations of institutionally mandated courses of action. The concepts developed in the Battered Women's Movement as they became incorporated institutionally were no longer a medium for expressing what women had been experiencing in their home lives. Walker describes how the concept of "family violence" became an "ordering procedure" for assembling (Walker, 1995, p. 75) reports and recommendations of a legislative standing committee.

> The new language displaces [women's] distinctive experiential orientation. The institutional concepts articulate to the functions of departments and committees as they were embedded in the formal standardizing language of the government authorization. (Walker, 1995, p. 95)

We have seen in the various studies described in this book just how the institutionally mandated textual representation becomes the operative "reality," displacing how things actually are for people. When we turned to studies directly oriented to making change, we have been shown by Ellen Pence how the professional language of the various professions – police, lawyers, social workers, probation officers, and so on – that are active in the judicial processing of "domestic abuse" precluded attending to what the victim might be going through. And we have already pointed out in the Six Nations exploration how "sexual violence" complaints are taken up and proceed and thus how the institutional language of Ontario law pre-empts police taking their own traditional culture and participation in the local community into account.

In a sense, the textually coordinated world of the ruling relations, of governance, of what we are pointing to using the concept of "institution" and so on, is one that displaces actualities while at the same time getting things done in the real world and having consequences there. In chapter 4 on "Discourse" we briefly described Paul Luken and Suzanne Vaughan's (2014) major study of a governmental discourse promoting a standardization of American housing, home ownership, and houses and furnishings for the best child-rearing. It was clearly a discourse designed to advance the value of suburban housing. Their use of the concept of discourse to reach beyond the housing experiences of the older women they interviewed in Phoenix is a model for how institutional ethnography can be used to open up major issues of societal change

In opening up the possibilities of the further reach of our sociology, Bob Jessop's use of the concept of imaginary is a useful metaphor: "[A]n imaginary is a semiotic ensemble (without tightly defined boundaries) that frames individual subjects' lived experience of an inordinately complex world and/or guides collective calculation about that world" (Jessop, 2014, p. 4). Those working as management, or making policies or government programs, or negotiating internationally (Eastwood, 2019), or otherwise active in text-coordinated governance, are stuck with imaginaries as they make their decisions. While we were engaged in this part of our developing conversations with institutional ethnography, Dorothy happened to read an article in *Le Monde diplomatique* about France's "yellow vest" movement, as it had then been developing over recent weeks. Though the movement emerged as a response to the imposition of a fuel tax, it had been the last straw in a sequence of government decisions that had increasingly depleted the resources of French workers. What could be seen was, in a sense, the pursuit by Emmanuel Macron's government of step-by-step moves that deprived workers of resources and supports:

> How did we let this happen? Thanks to the yellow vests, everyone is more aware of the government's injustices: €5 a month less in 2017 for housing benefit while the progressive rates of tax on capital were abolished; the wealth tax eliminated; pensioners' purchasing power declining. The costliest measure was the replacement of the tax credit for competitiveness and employment ... with a reduction in employers' social security contributions. (Halimi, 2019, p. 2)

If we connect again with Rankin and Campbell's study *Managing to Nurse*, we can see how the local actualities of work at ground level as they are entered into the accountability circuits of management are represented – at the managerial level – in the selective organization that enables them to be assessed monetarily. In the institutional settings of governance, there will be those who read the textual representations in terms of their relevance for possible governing actions – for example, at the national level, designing the policies for an annual budget, which was likely part of how Macron and his administration assembled the various costs to workers that were imposed. Using the text-based representations of the monetary status of the various government functions, estimates could be made of the budgetary payoffs of the various moves. Here are possibilities for institutional ethnographic explorations of Jessop's "economic imaginaries":

> The totality of economic activities is so unstructured and complex that it cannot be an object of calculation, management, governance, or guidance. Instead such practices are always oriented to subsets of economic relations (economic systems or subsystems) that have been discursively and, perhaps organizationally and institutionally, fixed as objects of intervention. This involves 'economic imaginaries' that rely on semiosis to constitute these subsets. Moreover ... these imaginaries must have some significant, albeit necessarily partial, correspondence to real material interdependencies in the actually existing economy and/or in relations between economic and extra-economic activities. (Jessop, 2014, p. 4)

More generally for institutional ethnographers, discovering institutional circuits begins to make visible a whole region of action built on the institutional language of governing texts that displace people's actualities. Of special relevance in contemporary Canada is what

Rankin and Campbell explored (see chapter 8) as the imposition of new managerialism practices on public services, elucidating how services are delivered to the monetary system of the capitalist economy.

For institutional ethnography, of course, the metaphor of "imaginaries" is not where we come to rest. Our project is discovering and making visible just how actual people are actually putting things together in coordinated sequences of action. In a sense, this is an invitation to institutional ethnographers to pass from Jessop's powerful metaphor to accounts of just what is getting done and how it is being put together. Here is a specimen of just such an exploration of how textual realities may be created that are detached from the local actualities in which they originate and become the "reality" on which action proceeds; it is part of Turner's account of making her map of a municipal process, of arriving at the moment of proceeding with the development of a site in a ravine familiar to local residents:

> The textual reality of the "site" stands in for the physical site. In the application to develop the wooded Howitt Park ravine, the physical land is described as "vacant land." The forms of "municipal knowing" already exist, are already constituted, and have their peculiar textual technologies. The forms are activated and reproduced each and every time, in every site development planning process. The land is described and becomes known in language, by numbers and mathematically drawn lines that stand in for the size and shape and contours of the physical land. (Turner, 2006, p. 148)

Although grounded in scientifically based technologies of measurement, etc., the textual reality of the site has become an imaginary. In a later paper, Turner (2014) draws on her recording of a city council meeting to show how a given map of the site was read very differently by the residents of the area, who knew well and referred to the actualities of the ravine they were familiar with; and by councillors, who read the map not as a map but as a *plan* and did not refer to what was actually there. This is not, of course, to suggest that the technologically sophisticated methods of representing abstracted properties of the site were inaccurate or fraudulent, but rather to bring into view an instance of the work–text organization of what becomes an "imaginary" as the original actualities disappear.

Explorations such as Turner's show the possibilities of institutional ethnography for engaging with a governing world grounded in representational texts constructed selectively from actualities; here are people at work who create and deploy the representations that coordinate courses of institutional action that actually happen. Staying always with what actual people are doing and how this is coordinated textually makes it possible to open up for ethnographic investigation just how such phenomena as Jessop locates with his metaphoric "imaginary" are actually being put together by actual people in actual local settings of their work. Institutional ethnography's recognition of texts as coordinating people's work and, increasingly, our recognition of language as integral to social organization, makes it possible to explore ruling relations ethnographically. There may be practical difficulties about reaching into the work worlds at levels of ruling in its various forms, but IE has research capacities to discover just how the world as we are living it now is being put together.

References

Arnup, K. (1994). *Education for motherhood: Education for mothers in twentieth-century Canada.* Toronto: University of Toronto Press.

Bakhtin, M.M. (1981). *The dialogic imagination: Four essays.* (M. Holquist, Ed.). Austin: University of Texas Press.

Bakhtin, M.M. (1986). *Speech genres and other late essays.* (C. Emerson and M. Holquist, Eds.). Austin: University of Texas Press.

Billig, M. (2013). *Learn to write badly: How to succeed in the social sciences.* Cambridge: Cambridge University Press.

Bourdieu, P. (1990). *The logic of practice.* Stanford, CA: Stanford University Press.

Bourdieu, P. (2000). To the reader. In P. Bourdieu et al. (Eds.), *The weight of the world: Social suffering in contemporary society*, 1–2. Trans. P.P. Ferguson, S. Emanuel, J. Johnson, and S.T. Waryn. Stanford, CA: Stanford University Press.

Bourdieu, P., et al. (Eds.). (2000). *The weight of the world: Social suffering in contemporary society.* Trans. P.P. Ferguson, S. Emanuel, J. Johnson, and S.T. Waryn. Stanford, CA: Stanford University Press.

Bresalier, M., Gillis, L., McClure, C., McCoy, L., Mykhalovskiy, E., Taylor, A., & Webber, M. (Eds.) (2002). *Making care visible: Antiretroviral therapy and the health work of people living with HIV/AIDS*, 37–63. Toronto: Making Care Visible Group.

Campbell, M.L. (2006). Institutional ethnography and experience as data. In D.E. Smith (Ed.), *Institutional ethnography as practice*, 91–107. Lanham, MD: Rowman and Littlefield.

Campbell, M.L., & Gregor, F.M. (2002). *Mapping social relations: A primer in doing institutional ethnography.* Lanham, MD: Rowman and Littlefield.

Campbell, M.L., & Manicom, A. (Eds.). (1995). *Knowledge, experience and ruling relations: Studies in the social organization of knowledge.* Toronto: University of Toronto Press.

Corman, M.K. (2017). *Paramedics on and off the streets: Emergency medical services in the age of technological governance.* Toronto: University of Toronto Press

Dalla Costa, M., & James, S. (1972). *The power of women and the subversion of the community.* London: Falling Wall Press.

Daniels, A.K. (1987). Invisible work. *Social Problems, 34*(5): 403–15.

Darville, R. (2014). Literacy work and the adult literacy regime. In A.I. Griffith and D.E. Smith (Eds.), *Under new public management: Institutional ethnographies of changing front-line work,* 25–57. Toronto: University of Toronto Press.

de Montigny, G.J. (1995). *Social working: An ethnography of front-line practice.* Toronto: University of Toronto Press.

de Montigny, G.J. (1995b). The power of being professional. In M.L. Campbell and A. Manicom (Eds.), *Knowledge, experience and ruling relations: Studies in the social organization of knowledge,* 209–20. Toronto: University of Toronto Press.

de Montigny, G.J. (2014). Doing child protection work. In D.E. Smith and S.M. Turner (Eds.), *Incorporating texts into institutional ethnographies,* 173–94. Toronto: University of Toronto Press.

DeVault, M.L. (1991). *Feeding the family: The social organization of caring as gendered work.* Chicago: University of Chicago Press.

De Vault, M.L., & McCoy, L. (2006). Institutional ethnography: Using interviews to investigate ruling relations. In D.E. Smith (Ed.), *Institutional ethnography as practice,* 15–44. Lanham, MD: Rowman and Littlefield.

De Vault, M.L., Venkatesh, M., & Ridzi, F. (2014). "Let's be friends:" Working within an accountability circuit. In A.I. Griffith and D.E. Smith (Eds.), *Under new public management: Institutional ethnographies of changing front-line work,* 177–98. Toronto: University of Toronto Press.

Deveau, J.L. (2014). Using institutional ethnography's ideological circle to portray how textually mediated disability discourse paralysed a Supreme Court of Canada ruling. *Culture and Organization, 22*(4): 311–29. https://doi.org/10.1080/14759551.2014.940042.

Diamond, T. (1992). *Making gray gold: Narratives of nursing home care.* Chicago: University of Chicago Press.

Eastwood, L.E. (2006). Making the institution ethnographically accessible: UN document production and the transformation of experience. In D.E. Smith (Ed.), *Institutional ethnography as practice,* 181–97. Lanham, MD: Rowman and Littlefield.

Eastwood, L.E. (2014). Negotiating UN policy: Activating texts in setting-specific policy deliberations. In D.E. Smith and Susan M. Turner (Eds.), *Texts in action: Exploring ruling relations ethnographically,* 64–90. Toronto: University of Toronto Press.

Eastwood, L.E. (2018). *Negotiating the environment: Civil society, globalisation, and the UN.* London: Routledge.

Foucault, M. (1970). *The order of things: An archaeology of the human sciences.* London: Tavistock.

Foucault, M. (1972). The discourse on language (appendix). *The archaeology of knowledge.* New York: Pantheon.

Foucault, M. (1981). The order of discourse. In R. Young (Ed.), *Untying the text: A poststructuralist reader,* 51–78. London: Routledge.

Gibson, J.W. (1986). *The perfect war: Technowar in Vietnam.* New York: Grove Atlantic.

Glazer, N. (1993). *Women's paid and unpaid labor: The work transfer in health care and retailing.* Philadelphia: Temple University Press.

Grahame, K.M. (1998). Asian women, job training, and the social organization of immigrant labor markets. *Qualitative Sociology, 21,* 72–90. https://doi .org/10.1023/A:1022123409995.

Griffith, A. (2006). Constructing single parent families for schooling: Discovering an institutional discourse. In D.E. Smith (Ed.), *Institutional ethnography as practice,* 127–38. Lanham, MD: Rowman and Littlefield.

Griffith, A.I., & Smith, D.E. (2005). *Mothering for schooling.* New York: Routledge.

Griffith, A.I., & Smith, D.E. (Eds.). (2014). *Under new public management: Institutional ethnographies of changing front-line work.* Toronto: University of Toronto Press.

Halimi, S. (2019). Forgotten France rises up. (George Miller, Trans.). *Le Monde diplomatique,* January, 2–3.

Janz, S. (2009). Accreditation and government contracted social service delivery in British Columbia: A reorganization of front-line social service work. Unpublished MA thesis, Victoria, BC: University of Victoria.

Jessop, B. (2014). Critical semiotic analysis and cultural political economy. https://bobjessop.wordpress.com/2014/12/15/critical-semiotic-analysis -and-cultural-political-economy/.

Kafka, B. (2012). *The demon of writing: Powers and failures of paperwork.* Brooklyn, NY: Zone.

Karnad-Jani, R. (2015). Silent voices: "South Asian" mothers and transition to high school: A decolonizing institutional ethnography of mothering work. Research paper submitted to the University of Toronto Faculty of Graduate Studies for completion of MEd degree.

Luken, P.C., & Vaughan, S. (2014). Standardizing childrearing through housing. In D.E. Smith and S.M. Turner (Eds.), *Incorporating texts into institutional ethnographies,* 255–304. Toronto: University of Toronto Press.

Luria, A.R. (1961). *The role of speech in the regulation of normal and abnormal behaviour.* New York: Pergamon.

Luria, A.R. (1976). *Cognitive development: Its cultural and social foundations.* Cambridge, MA: Harvard University Press.

Luria, A.R., & Yudovich, F. La. (1971). *Speech and the development of mental processes in the child*. New York: Penguin.

Marx, K. (1973). *Grundrisse: Foundations of the critique of political economy*. (M. Nicolaus, Trans.). New York: Vintage.

Marx, K. (1976). *Capital: A critique of political economy*. London: Penguin.

Marx, K., & Engels, F. (1973). *Feuerbach: Opposition of the materialist and idealist outlooks*. London: Lawrence and Wishart.

Marx, K., & Engels, F. (1976). *The German ideology*. Moscow: Progress.

McCoy, L. (1999). *Accounting discourse and textual practices of ruling: A study of institutional transformation and restructuring in higher education*. PhD diss., Toronto: University of Toronto.

McCoy, L. (2002). Dealing with doctors. In M. Bresalier, L. Gillis, C. McClure, L. McCoy, E. Mykhalovskiy, D. Taylor, and M. Webber (Eds.), *Making care visible: Antiretroviral therapy and the health work of people living with HIV/AIDS*, 1–36. Toronto: Making Care Visible Group.

Mishler, E.G. (1986). *Research interviewing: Context and narrative*. Cambridge, MA: Harvard University Press.

Mykhaloskiy, E. (2002). Understanding the social character of treatment decision-making. In M. Bresalier, L. Gillis, C. McClure, L. McCoy, E. Mykhalovskiy, A. Taylor, and M. Webber (Eds.), *Making care visible: Antiretroviral therapy and the health work of people living with HIV/AIDS*, 37–63. Toronto: Making Care Visible Group.

Mykhaloskiy, E. (2008). Beyond decision making: Class, community organizations and the healthwork of people living with HIV/AIDS. Contributions from Institutional Ethnographic Research. *Medical anthropology: Cross cultural studies in health and illness*, 27(2): 136–63. https://doi.org/10.1080/01459740802017363.

Mykhaloskiy, E., and L. McCoy. (2002). Troubling ruling discourses of health: Using institutional ethnography in community-based research. *Critical Public Health*, 12(1): 17–37. https://doi.org/10.1080/09581590110113286.

Pence, E. (1996). *Safety for battered women in a textually mediated legal system*. PhD diss., Toronto: University of Toronto.

Pence, E. (2001). Safety for battered women in a textually mediated legal system. *Studies in Cultures, Organizations, and Societies*, 7(2): 199–229. https://doi.org/10.1080/10245280108523558.

Pence, E., & Sadusky, J.M. (2005). *The praxis safety and accountability audit tool kit*. Duluth, MN: Praxis International.

Pence, E., & Smith, D.E. (2011). Institutional analysis: Making change from below. Presentation, Society for the Study of Social Problems, Annual Meeting, Las Vegas, Nevada.

Praxis International. (2020). Mission and history. https://praxisinternational.org/praxis-international-2/mission-and-history-2/.

Rankin, J.M. (1998). Health care reform and restructuring of nursing in British Columbia. Paper presented at Exploring the Restructuring and Transformation of Institutional Processes: Applications of Institutional Ethnography, York University, Toronto, October.

Rankin, J.M. (2001). Texts in action: How nurses are doing the fiscal work of health care reform. *Studies in Cultures, Organizations, and Societies*, 7(2): 251–67. https://doi.org/10.1080/10245280108523560.

Rankin, J.M., & Campbell, M.L. (2006). *Managing to nurse: Inside Canada's health care reform*. Toronto: University of Toronto Press.

Ryle, G. (1949). *The concept of mind*. London: Routledge.

Schmid, H.-J. (2000). *English abstract nouns as conceptual shells: From corpus to cognition*. Berlin: Mouton de Gruyter.

Schoenborn, D., Kuhn, T.R., & Karreman, D. (2019). The communicative constituent of organization, organizing, and organizationality. *Organizational Studies*, Vol. 40, 4.475–96. https://doi.org/10.1177/0170840618782284.

Scott, W.R. (1995). *Institutions and organizations*. Thousand Oaks, CA: Sage.

Sechehaye, M. (1994). *The autobiography of a schizophrenic girl: The true story of Renee*. New York: Meridian.

Shepard, M.F., & Pence, E.L. (1999). *Coordinating community responses to domestic violence: Lessons from Duluth and beyond*. Duluth and St. Paul, MN: Praxis International.

Smith, D.E. (1963). *Power and the front line: Social controls in a state mental hospital*. PhD diss., Berkeley: University of California.

Smith, D.E. (1974). The ideological practice of sociology. *Catalyst, 8*(Winter): 39–54.

Smith, D.E. (1984). Textually mediated social organization. *International Journal of Sociology, 36*(1): 59–75.

Smith, D.E. (1987). *The everyday world as problematic: A feminist sociology*. Toronto: University of Toronto Press.

Smith, D.E. (2001). Texts and the ontology of institutions and organizations. *Studies in Cultures, Organizations, and Societies*, 7(2): 159–48. https://doi.org/10.1080/10245280108523557.

Smith, D.E. (2004). Ideology, science, and social relations: A reinterpretation of Marx's epistemology. *European Journal of Social Theory, 7*(1): 445–62. https://doi.org/10.1177/1368431004046702.

Smith, D.E. (2016). Exploring words as people's practices. In J. Lynch, J Rowlands, T. Gale, and A. Skourdoumbis (Eds.), *Diffractive readings in practice: Trajectories in theory, fields and professions*, 23–38. London: Routledge.

Smith, D.E., & Dobson, S. (2011). Storing and transmitting skills: The expropriation of working-class control. In D.W. Livingstone, D.E. Smith, and W. Smith (Eds.), *Manufacturing meltdown: Reshaping steelwork*, 79–147. Winnipeg: Fernwood.

Smith, D.E., & Turner, S. (Eds.). (2014). *Incorporating texts into institutional ethnographies*. Toronto: University of Toronto Press.

Smith, G.W. (1988). Policing the gay community: An inquiry into textually mediated relations. *International Journal of Sociology and the Law, 16*: 163–83.

Smith, G.W. (1990). Political activist as ethnographer. *Social Problems, 37*: 401–21. https://doi.org/10.1525/sp.1990.37.4.03a00140.

Smith, G.W. (1995). Accessing treatments: Managing the AIDS epidemic in Toronto. In M. Campbell and A. Manicom (Eds.), *Knowledge, experience, and ruling relations: Essays in the social organization of knowledge*, 18–34. Toronto: University of Toronto Press.

Smith, G.W. (1998). The ideology of "fag:" Barriers to education for gay students. *Sociological Quarterly, 39*(2): 309–35. https://doi.org/10.1111/j.1533-8525.1998.tb00506.x.

Smith, G.W., Mykhalovskiy, E., & Weatherbee, D. (2006). Getting "hooked up": An organizational study of the problems people with HIV/AIDS have accessing social services. In D.E. Smith (Ed.), *Institutional ethnography as practice*, 166–79. Lanham, MD: Rowman and Littlefield.

Turner, S.M. (2001). Texts and the institutions of municipal planning government: The power of texts in the public process of land development. *Studies in Cultures, Organizations, and Societies, 7*(2): 297–325. https://doi.org/10.1080/10245280108523562.

Turner, S.M. (2003). *The social organization of planning: A study of institutional actions as texts and work processes*. PhD diss., Toronto: University of Toronto.

Turner, S.M. (2006). Mapping institutions as work and text. In D.E. Smith (Ed.), *Institutional ethnography as practice*, 131–62. Lanham, MD: Rowman and Littlefield.

Turner, S.M. (2014). Reading practices in decision processes. In D.E. Smith & S.M. Turner (eds), *Incorporating texts into institutional ethnographies*, 197–224. Toronto: University of Toronto Press.

Turner, S.M., Bomberry, J., & Werner, A. (2017). *On-reserve First Nations police reporting, responses and support services, and investigative practices*. Toronto, Ministry of Community Safety and Correctional Services, Ontario Police Responses to Sexual Violence Against Aboriginal Women and Girls, 2015–2016 Program.

Walker, G.A. (1990). *Family violence and the women's movement: The conceptual politics of struggle*. Toronto: University of Toronto Press.

Walker, G.A. (1995). Violence and the relations of ruling: Lessons from the battered women's movement. In M. Campbell and A. Manicom (Eds.), *Knowledge, experience and ruling relations: Studies in the social organization of management*, 65–79. Toronto: University of Toronto Press.

Waters, N. (2015). Towards an institutional counter-cartography of nurses' wound work. *Journal of Sociology and Social Welfare, 62*(June): 127–56.

Wikipedia. (2020). *Mass production*. https://en.wikipedia.org/wiki/Mass_production.

Index